P9-CEF-222

Building Men Who Matter

On the Marvel and Mystery of Raising Teenage Boys

Brother James M. Kelly, C.F.X.

Butler Books
Louisville

ISBN 978-1-935497-31-8

Printed in Canada

Book design by Eric Butler
Cover design by Scott Stortz

PUBLISHED BY:

Butler Books
P.O. Box 7311
Louisville, KY 40207
(502) 897–9393
Fax (502) 897–9797
www.butlerbooks.com

In Memory of My Parents
Joseph Patrick Kelly
and
Dorothy Vigneault Kelly

and

In Loving Gratitude to My Sister
Patricia Mary Kelly

Table of Contents

Preface ix

Section One—The Final Years at Saint Xavier High School (1998–2001)

On the Oblivious Nature of the Adolescent Male 3
More on Vigilance 6
On Repetition as the Mother of Learning 10
On the Memorare and Intercessory Prayer 12
On Leading the Horse to Water 15
On Praise and Patience 18
On Grandparents 21
On Sister Miriam Patricia and Cheating 25
On Winston Churchill and Parenting 29
On Dobie the Saint Bernard and Finding the Right Garden 33
On Letting Go 37
On Athletics and Perspective 41
On Teenage Boys and the Things That Don't Change 45
On Training Puppies 49
On Being Careful With Our Words 53
On Saying Goodbye 57

Section Two—Mount Saint Joseph (2001–Present)

On the Ingredients of Good Parenting 63
On Telling the Truth 65
On Mixed Signals 69

On Humor and Proportion 72
On Nice Boys and Laziness 75
On Appearance and Reality 78
On Adolescent Time Schedules 81
On Good Parenting, Good Schooling and God's Grace 84
On Rogue Male Elephants 87
On Wise Fools and Parental Endurance 90
On Electronic Leashes and Parental Surveillance 93
On Cold Winters and Warm Memories 97
On Recognizing Contrition 100
On Opening the Door 104
On Blessings and Curses 107
On Aunts and the Resurrection 110
On Butterflies and Letting Go 114
On Having a Heart in the Right Place 116
On Young Love 118
On Humility 121
On Family Dinners 124
On Saint Joseph and God in the Messy Details of Life 128
On Testing the Limits 131
On Taking the Keys 134
On Having No Regrets 137
On Good Advice and the Young 140
On Understanding Our Parents 143
On Growing Up 146
On Unfathomable Mysteries 149
On Jerome and Perspective 152
On Holding on to Faith 155
On Finding the Right Balance 158
On a Spring Afternoon at the Mount 161
On the Adolescent Journey 164
On the Spectrum of Faith 167
On the Subjunctive of Attraction 170

On Listening Children 173
On Some Aspects of the Nature of the Teenage Male 176
On Things We'd Rather Forget 179
On Getting Involved 181
On Giving Good Example 184
An Autumnal Reflection 187
On Differing Perspectives 190
On Haircuts and Adolescent Rebellion 193
On Boys as Barometers 196
On Churchill and Expectations 199
More on Motivation 202
In Praise of Praise 205
On God the Father and My Father 208

SECTION THREE—MOTHERS AND SONS

On Saint Monica and a Mother's Prayer 213
On Mothers and Grandmothers 216
On Good Mothers and Clean Underwear 219
On Eternal Bonds 222
On Cousin Honey and Mothers 225

SECTION FOUR—THE XAVERIAN BROTHERS

On Brother Paul and 150 Years 231
On Xaverian Education and Good Role Models 235
On Brother Lambert and a Xaverian Education 239
On Brother Eric, Brother Carlos and Xaverian Education 243
On the Continuing Legacy of the Mount 247
On Brother Declan and Ashes to Easter 251
On Brother Dominic and One Hundred and Thirty Years 254
On Brothers Hilary and Rudolph and the
Unchanging Nature of the Teenage Male 258
On Brother Terence and Humility 262
On Brother Kevin and Motivation 265

Section Five—Advent and Christmas

On Advent 271
On Preparing the Way of the Lord 274
On Advent and Not Missing the Moment 276
On the Inscrutable Providence of God 278
On Advent and Slowing Down 281
Christmas 1995 284
Christmas 1998 286
Christmas 2001 288
Christmas 2002 291
Christmas 2003 293
Christmas 2004 295
Christmas 2005 297
Christmas 2006 299
Christmas 2007 301
Christmas 2008 303
Christmas 2009 305

Epilogue 307

PREFACE

In the preface for *Respecting the Man the Boy Will Become*, I quoted the old Irish adage, "Never let the truth get in the way of a good story." Since that time, I have actually become an Irish citizen through my paternal grandparents, both of whom were born in County Clare. At heart I am an Irish storyteller. The boys I have taught over the years could attest to the fact that I have stories for everything, stories to illustrate every point in English literature and stories to relate that literature to life.

Beginning my teaching career at Saint John's High School in Shrewsbury, Massachusetts in 1971, I have had the privilege to teach in the three oldest Xaverian Brothers high schools in the United States: Saint Xavier in Louisville, Kentucky, Mount Saint Joseph in Baltimore, Maryland and Saint John's High School in Shrewsbury, Massachusetts. I have also had the great privilege to serve as the Headmaster for our two oldest schools, Saint Xavier and Mount Saint Joseph. I also served as the Headmaster of one of our youngest schools, Xavier High School in Middletown, Connecticut. Xaverian education is at the very core of my being. I wouldn't know how to administer or teach apart from that tradition. The corporate wisdom of the Xaverian Brothers, passed down to me from some legendary Xaverians, informs everything I do, everything I write and everything I say. When *Respecting the Man the Boy Will Become* was published and was a success far beyond my imagination, it was suggested to me that it could become a national bestseller if I could edit out God and the Xaverian Brothers. To that I replied, "Why don't you just rip my heart out?" We Xaverian Brothers educate in faith: "Everything with God, nothing without God."

Mount Saint Joseph is presently engaged in a Capital Campaign, the motto for which is *Building Men Who Matter.* That phrase sums up quite succinctly what Xaverian education, at least at our all-male schools, attempts to do. It is what every parent of a son attempts to do. I hope what is written here serves as an encouragement for parents doing their best to raise sons who will become men who matter.

Of course, I can't publish again without thanking profoundly the ladies in my life. Mrs. Doris Dolle and Mrs. Rita Dunham-Turek at Saint X and Mrs. Cindy Drenner and Mrs. Mary Ellen Dolan at Mount Saint Joseph have devoted months and years to typing the complete works of Kelly. Without their daily help and support, I would be completely lost. Behind this man there have been four good women. Actually, five! The late Claire Nellis, my first secretary at Xavier High School, taught me more about running a school than any education course or professional mentor could ever have done. Her wisdom and common sense guided me in my first principalship. Thanks, as well, to Brother Thomas Ryan, C.F.X., a master grammarian, who has been proofing my work for years, and to Mr. Bern McDivitt, who took on the challenge of proofing the final manuscript for this project. He has the last word! A special thanks to Mrs. Rita Dunham-Turek for the yeoman's work she has done editing and proofing this manuscript. When I left

Saint X in 2001, she told me that she wanted to be involved in the second book. Involved she is!

And as for the old Irish adage . . . What I write here is true, yet while all of my stories are based on fact, I play with the details to preserve anonymity and to ensure the smooth flow of the narrative. I hope you find my Irish storytelling helpful.

SECTION ONE

THE FINAL YEARS AT SAINT XAVIER HIGH SCHOOL 1998–2001

On the Oblivious Nature of the Adolescent Male

If you have ever tried to pilot your car up the front driveway at St. X when classes are changing, you have had a first-hand experience of the oblivious nature of the adolescent male. Although you may be driving a large sport utility vehicle, which is hard to miss, you will quickly discover that the students pay absolutely no attention to your efforts to drive through this adolescent multitude. As they completely block your way, they will look right at you and smile. This is not rudeness. It is oblivion. They are either talking to their friends, thinking about their latest life crisis or planning their excuse for missing homework for the next teacher. You and your car have not registered on their reality screen. In despair, you will finally give up and wait for the passing period to end before you go on your way.

I don't need to tell you that adolescents go through a period of complete self-absorption. The good news is that they grow out of it, but while they're in it, this stage can be somewhat maddening for parents. Your son is oblivious to so many things. He's oblivious to the chaos of his room and the chaos he might leave scattered about the house as his belongings creep out of his room. He's oblivious to the havoc that his failure to think ahead and to plan ahead can wreak on family plans and on the lives of the other members of his family. Most of all, he can be oblivious to the effect that his actions and words have on the feelings of others. He might be hypersensitive about his own feelings, but when it comes to the feelings of others, he simply doesn't register them in his mind. This does not mean that he is going to grow up to be an insensitive and uncaring father and husband. It simply means that he's being a typical teenage male.

I have mentioned to you before that our Christian Awakening Retreat in the junior year can be, although not always, a wake-up call for a boy about his own oblivion to the feelings and needs of others. Any adult in the St. X community who has worked on these retreats can tell you a multitude of stories of boys who suddenly discover how shabbily they have been treating their parents, their siblings and their friends. This shabby treatment has far more to do with oblivion than it does with bad will. Teenage boys are so absorbed in themselves that they don't focus on how their words and their actions affect others. When they finally recognize this, they really begin to grow up. Our retreat closings are usually peppered with apologies to parents from boys who have finally realized that they have taken their parents for granted, and that their parents have endured this shabby treatment while they patiently waited for their sons to grow up.

Another sad wake-up call for the teenage male is when one of his friends loses a parent. I recall a time in Connecticut when three boys in the junior class lost their fathers within three weeks. We saw an incredible change in the junior class in the time after those deaths. All of a sudden we had 200 boys who were actually contemplating what life would be like without their fathers and who, for at least a few weeks after those deaths, were incredibly considerate of their fathers. Of course, the insight didn't last as long as we would have liked.

If your son is in a stage of high oblivion, don't worry too much about it. It will pass. Gradually, he will recognize that there is a world around him and that other people have feelings just as he does. Of course, it won't pass completely since there is some oblivion that just goes with being a man. Ten years from now his wife will be telling him, just as his mother does now, that he really should write a thank-you note to his grandmother for the birthday gift she sent him six months ago. Since women tend not to be oblivious, they can serve as a good reality check for the men in their lives. My godson is a rather dilatory writer of thank-you notes and, for years, his mother made sure that he thanked me whenever I sent him a gift. Now his lovely wife, Tracy, has taken over that task. Of course, I would never remember to send birthday cards and gifts to him or to anyone else unless my lovely secretary, Mrs. Dolle, didn't remind me. She keeps careful track of my calendar and reminds me four or five times before any occasion when I need to send a card or a gift. Oblivious teenage males do become less oblivious as time goes on. Just don't hope for a total transformation!

More On Vigilance

At least once a year I write you a letter which is a departure from my usual style. No stories and no humor. This is that letter for this school year.

Whenever I am out in the community or traveling the country to visit our far-flung alumni and anyone asks how things are going at St. X, I reply, "At the moment, they're fine." If you work with 1,500 teenage boys, you learn very early that you live from moment to moment. At any moment of any day, one of the 1,500 young men at St. X can be guilty of a major error in judgment and common sense. We have a wonderful student body here, and I love them dearly, but they aren't saints. They are teenage boys and, as teenage boys, they bring to school with them the everyday problems of the world in which they live. As a result, they occasionally can get themselves into a good bit of trouble. We have boys at St. X from every zip code in Louisville and from the seven surrounding counties. We have boys at St. X from every conceivable family structure. Given all of that, we, as a school, are as vigilant as we can possibly be and, when trouble arises, we act quickly and, hopefully, in the best interest of the entire student body.

I had thought to list for you every conceivable problem that can arise when you deal with teenage boys, but I think you already know that list. If it can happen to a teenage boy, it can happen at St. X. We are aware of that, and we keep our eyes open. For example, you know that we are very vigilant about drug and alcohol abuse. We've had the drug dog on several occasions, and we will have the drug dog again. Drugs, unfortunately, have become part of adolescent life. We have also been very vigilant about gangs and, while we don't perceive a problem with that in school at the moment, we know that some St. X boys have been involved in such activity outside of school. You are no doubt well aware that teenage boys mistakenly think that they are immortal and, as a result, their driving at times can be rather reckless. When we hear of a boy driving recklessly, we act immediately. You have perhaps noticed that the traffic lights on Poplar Level Road are not synchronized. This was done deliberately to get St. X boys to slow down. This non-synchronization of the traffic lights goes back decades to when the fathers of the present student body were students at St. X. While many things in the world have changed since that time, the nature of the beast hasn't changed and, as I've told you many times before, unless you understand perfectly the nature of the beast, you can't help the beast grow into a mature, Christian gentleman.

I think we're pretty honest about the potential for good and for the not so good among our students. We do ask boys, on occasion, to leave the school. There are times when we simply don't have any choice, but I hope that we always act in a Christian manner. There are many times when Dr. Sangalli, in administering discipline, has to consider the good of 1,500 students over the good of one. That's justice, and justice is still Christian. Early on in my career, a very wise principal once told me that the principal of a Catholic high school will always experience a tension between mercy and justice and that, at times, the most merciful thing to do is to be absolutely just. It may sound contradictory, but I've found it to be quite true and quite good advice.

As parents, you need to be as aware as you can possibly be of the potential for trouble in the teenage male. That doesn't mean that you have to mistrust your son or suspect that he's always up to no good, but you do have to keep your eyes open. Teenage boys can get in over their heads so quickly that to say that it happens "in the blink of an eye" is an understatement. Keep your eyes and your ears open. We'll do the same at school. If you hear anything that you think we need to know, please call us. If we see anything in your son that we think you need to know, we'll call you. You need to remember that we have a "zero tolerance" drug policy at St. X. In most instances, a boy will get one or two strikes before he's out, but with reference to any drug-related offense, it's one strike, and there is no reprieve.

On those days when things are not going well and when I begin to get discouraged about our success at damming the flood of adolescent potential, I console myself by remembering something I've learned very clearly over my twenty-seven years as a school teacher and my fifteen years as a headmaster. The work of education, at home and at school, depends far more on God than it does on parents and school teachers. We prepare the soil, plant the seeds and water them, but it is God who gives the growth. More and more I've come to realize how little depends on me and how much depends on God. Saint Paul reminds us that God can do "infinitely more than we can ask or imagine." Not long ago, a young alumnus who gave me more than a few gray hairs during his tenure at St. X stopped by to tell me that he had decided to become a school teacher so that he could give back some of what he had been given. His parents and St. X planted those seeds, but it was certainly God who gave the growth.

Every school day, 1,508 young men come into this building and 99% of them do their work, follow the rules and really want to make the school and their parents proud of them. The 1% who don't on a given day are usually not the 1% who didn't the day before or won't the day after! The goodwill is there and, with some coaxing and cajoling from their parents and teachers—and, most importantly, with God's grace—they will become men of whom their parents, their teachers, St. Xavier, and God can be proud.

On Repetition as the Mother of Learning

If you have any hope of getting through to the oblivious nature of the teenage male, you have to become somewhat like a broken record. Because teenage boys tend to tune adults out, you have to hope that, at least one time out of the ninety-nine times that you tell your son something or give him some advice, he'll actually be listening and hear what you say. That is why repetition is the mother of learning. If it's worth saying once to a teenage boy, it's worth saying 1,000 times. After saying it 999 times, he might just get it. Years ago, I had a teacher in high school who was the most repetitious woman I had ever met. I used to wonder if she thought that we were all either deaf or stupid. I realize now that she was just a seasoned school teacher who understood that teenagers, male and female, aren't always terribly attentive.

In the century before Christ, the Roman senator Cato ended every speech to the Roman senate with, "Carthage must be destroyed." Cato apparently thought that, if he said it enough, the other senators might finally get the point. If your son occasionally listens to my Monday morning pep talk, he can tell you that I believe firmly in the Cato philosophy because I repeat two themes, frequently ending my talks with, "Wear your seat belts!" In the second semester, I add a second message which I direct to the seniors, a message which reflects the sad fact that, every year, at least one second-semester senior manages to get himself expelled from school by doing something very stupid. I tell them, "You've been here three-and-a-half years. You like St. X, and we like you. Don't do anything stupid between now and May which would jeopardize your graduation and break your mother's and your grandmother's heart."

When you attempt to give your son good advice, he'll insist that he's heard you and, if you repeat it, he will roll his eyes and give you that "you poor, pitiful adult" look which adolescent males love to give their teachers and their parents. Believe me when I tell you that he probably has not really heard what you've said and that you need to repeat it frequently and with all the drama you can manage. My hero, Winston Churchill, once said that if a book isn't worth reading twice, it wasn't worth reading once. I say that if parental advice isn't worth giving a thousand times, it wasn't worth giving once.

Even when they do listen, sometimes teenage boys can get the message confused. A few years ago I was at the hospital bedside of a young man who had been in a wreck and who had not been wearing his seat belt. Thank God he was not seriously injured. Always a school teacher, I said, "What have I told you a thousand times?" He replied immediately, "That I shouldn't break my mother's and my grandmother's heart between now and graduation!" To that I replied, ". . . which you certainly would have done if you had gotten yourself killed because you weren't wearing your seat belt."

Remember that if it's worth saying once, it's worth saying 1,000 times, even if your son gets it all backwards. It just may be that on the 1,000th time he actually hears you and that keeps him alive and out of trouble.

On the Memorare and Intercessory Prayer

> Remember, O most gracious Virgin Mary, that never was it known that anyone who fled to your protection, implored your help or sought your intercession was left unaided. Inspired by this confidence, I fly unto you, O virgin of virgins, my mother! To you do I come, before you I stand, sinful and sorrowful. O mother of the Word Incarnate, despise not my petitions, but in your clemency hear and answer them. Amen.
>
> The Memorare of St. Bernard of Clairvaux

I've heard it said that you have to be forty-seven years old or older to remember the Catholic Church in its full pre-Vatican II rigor. That fact surprised me somewhat because I always assumed that our present parents have the same memories of the Church that I do. As I get older, I notice how much younger our parents look every year. Not long ago, I asked a man if he had come to school to pick up his brother. He replied, "No, Brother, I've come to pick up my son." I felt incredibly old!

My age and memories of the Church notwithstanding, Catholic doctrine has not changed, although our expression of that doctrine has become more modern than the cut-and-dried questions and answers of the *Baltimore Catechism*. The Church has always believed firmly in the power of intercessory prayer. Every time we attend Mass, we say in the Creed that we believe in "the communion of the saints, the resurrection of the body and life everlasting." We believe that those who have gone before us can be intercessors for us before the throne of God and that their intercession can be highly efficacious. I'm a firm believer in the communion of the saints. While I pray to the official canonized saints of the Church, most of my heavenly intercessors are not officially canonized. They are the many relatives, friends and Brothers who have gone before me and are now with the Lord. When I feel St. X is really in need of some particular grace, I go out to the Brothers' cemetery and pray to those Brothers buried there, many of whom gave many years of their lives to St. X. I particularly entrust the care of the school to Brother Conrad Callahan, Principal of St. X from 1965 to 1971, and to Brother James Leo McCarthy (Brother Howard) who gave twenty-seven years of his life to St. X. There's an old Catholic adage, "Work as if everything depended on you and pray as if everything depended on God." We work very hard every day at St. X to make sure that it is the best school possible and that it is faithfully fulfilling the mission for which Brother Paul founded it 134 years ago. I would like to think, however, that some of our present success has a great deal to do with the heavenly intercession of Brother Conrad and Brother James McCarthy.

Every year, I say the opening prayer at the first meeting of the MOMS Club. Creature of habit that I am, I always begin with the same prayer, the Memorare of St. Bernard. It seems appropriate to begin a meeting of mothers with a prayer to the Mother of God. Many mothers chime right in and say the prayer with me while others are probably hearing the prayer for the first time. That's when I really recognize the fact that I might be a Catholic of a different generation from our parents. The Memorare is my favorite prayer and, good Catholic that I am, I always go first to the Mother of God. There's an old Irish Catholic adage, "When you really need God's attention, you get His Mother to get it for you." Now, I'm sure some theologians might quibble with that, given our basic belief in God's ever-providential love, but on a practical level, I think I've seen the truth of the old adage.

At the close of one MOMS meeting after I had used the Memorare, a mother came up to me and told me a story about her son and the prayer. I can't remember the details exactly, but her son had either been in an accident or was seriously ill. Whatever the case, he was transported to the hospital in an ambulance, and she was with him in the ambulance. She told me, "He was so sick, and I was so helpless. I couldn't think what to do, so I said the Memorare over and over. 'Remember, O most gracious Virgin Mary, that never was it known that anyone who fled to your protection, implored your help or sought your intercession was left unaided.' My son recovered."

When the Xaverian Brothers went to England in 1848, they reintroduced the May Procession to English Catholics. England was not a very Catholic-friendly place at the time, but the Brothers traditionally had great devotion to the Blessed Virgin and wanted to spread that devotion. Since we are in the month of May, the month which the Church particularly dedicates to Mary, I'd like to suggest that, if you haven't prayed to her in a while, you begin to do so. After all, the power of intercessory prayer is one of those unchanging beliefs of the Church, and most mothers have a way of making their sons do what they want. Praying to God's mother just makes good Catholic sense!

On Leading the Horse to Water

In the Broadway musical *Mame*, the lead character, Mame Dennis, sings a song which captures beautifully the dilemma facing anyone who has to raise a child. Mame has had to raise her nephew and, at a point in the play when he's about to marry a girl who is obviously wrong for him, Mame wonders if his lack of good sense is her fault. She asks:

> Did he need a stronger hand?
> Did he need a lighter touch?
> Was I soft or was I tough?
> Did I give enough?
> Did I give too much?
> At the moment when he needed me,
> did I ever turn away?
> Should I blame the times I pampered him,
> or blame the times I bossed him?
> What a shame!
> I never really found the boy
> before I lost him.
> Would I make the same mistakes
> if he walked into my life today?

Mame's questions are the very real questions of a parent. If my son makes a mess of his life or his algebra grade, is it my fault? Did I put too much pressure on him or not quite enough? Where does my responsibility end and his begin?

The old adage, "You can lead a horse to water, but you can't make him drink," is a very appropriate answer to such parental questions. Your responsibility is to lead the horse to water. Having been led there, your son (the horse) has to do the drinking. You can't do it for him. If he's a stubborn horse who refuses to drink, it's not your fault. Pampering, bossing, strong hand, light hand, scolding, praising—all of these are means which any parent uses to get the horse to water. God only knows what the perfect blend of these elements looks like. Your own parents probably didn't find it and, most likely, neither will you.

In his letter this month, Dr. Sangalli outlines for you some practical steps that you, as parents, can take to lead your son to water. You can't force him to study, but you can see that he has the proper environment and the appropriate ground rules to facilitate study should he decide to put his mind to it. If junior can't talk to his girlfriend for three hours on the phone at night, then perhaps he might just use those three hours to pound German or French or physics into his head. If you take Dr. Sangalli's advice and set the stage for your son's academic success, you have fulfilled your obligations and have led the horse to water. The rest is up to the horse.

At the last judgment, God is obviously going to ask you if you fulfilled responsibly your duties as a parent. I would like to suggest that, when you stand before the throne of God, He is not going to ask you if your son became a doctor or a derelict. I suspect that He's going to ask you if you did your best to lead the horse to water.

Please pray for the faculty as we begin this school year. They have the formidable task of trying to lead 1,500 young men to water. I'll pray for you as you attempt to do the same with your son. Let's all pray that the horses have the good sense to drink!

On Praise and Patience

Shortly after the graduation of the Class of 1998, I received a letter from one of the graduates whom I had taught in English during his junior year. The young man was one of the finest students I have taught, and I very much value his talent and his opinion. The letter was basically a thank-you note which also offered me some suggestions about my teaching style.

Since I have the luxury of teaching only one class, I correct student essays very thoroughly, and I give each of my students an audiotape with suggestions as to how he can revise his essay to make it better. The kids jokingly say that I not only yell at them in class but at home as well. I firmly believe that good writing doesn't just happen. A student will only become a decent writer if he is willing to submit his work to constructive criticism and to revise his essay until it is really good. I learned this method from my own senior English teacher in high school. After we had written an essay, Sister Mary Hughita would have each member of the class stand up and read his or her essay. She would then say to the class, "All right, boys and girls, criticize." Sister Hughita did "peer review" of writing thirty years before it became the thing to do in education. Inevitably, when I read my essay, Sister Hughita would modify her instructions to, "All right, boys and girls, criticize ruthlessly." It was painful, but it helped me learn how to write.

I still submit everything which I write for publication to two very critical editors, so I can tell my students that I suffer along with them in the writing process. My former student said that he learned to write well because I was so critical of his writing and because I offered him ways of improving his writing. So far, so good.

The young man went on, however, to tell me that, while my criticism of students' work did indeed help them to improve their writing style, I did not take sufficient time to praise them when they did well. He also mentioned that I can be incredibly impatient when students aren't hitting the mark I have set for them. He put this all very politely within the context of my own philosophy of writing: You learn more from criticism than you do from anything else. The sad thing is that he didn't tell me anything which I didn't already know and which I hadn't worked sufficiently hard to improve. It did, however, touch me very deeply that he cared enough to take me at my word and to offer me suggestions. He concluded with, "Please take this letter as a sign of my care and concern for you and your continued success as a teacher, and don't change too much. Thank you for a wonderful experience at St. X."

I took this letter very much in the spirit in which he had written it, and I learned once again how much I can learn from my students. I suspect that you, as parents, have had similar experiences. There is some incredible wisdom swirling about in the maelstrom of the male adolescent. They have difficulty articulating their insights, but if you listen carefully, you can sense the wisdom. Sometimes they can articulate it quite clearly as my former student did in his letter to me.

Praise and patience! As with teaching the art of writing,

so with life. We probably all would do better and would be more effective as school teachers and as parents if we were more patient and if we took more time to praise.

Patience has never been my strong suit, and I suspect that I'm probably a little too old to change that significantly. I do think that I can learn to praise my students more when they do well, or at least to couch my criticism in terms which help them see the good work they have done even as I suggest ways to improve. I'm going to try to take "praise and patience" as my personal themes for this school year. Perhaps you could join me and take these themes in your parenting of your son. Then we can both pray for each other that God will help us to make these themes a reality in our lives.

On Grandparents

One of the great regrets of my life is that I did not really know my grandparents. While my maternal grandmother lived until I was sixteen, she was senile for the last few years of her life. Even before that, she spoke very little English and I spoke no French. I don't ever remember having a conversation with her. My other grandparents died when I was very young. I particularly regret not knowing my father's father after whom I am named. I've heard it said that the father-son relationship is always tricky, but if there is an Irish gene involved, it's impossible. My grandfather managed the impossible because, until the day his sons (my father and my uncle Fran) died, they worshipped their father's memory. When my father was in his eighties and my uncle in his seventies, I used to join them occasionally for lunch at one of their favorite watering holes. At these "Kelly boys" get-togethers, my dad and my uncle would tell me stories about the family and their youth. Whenever they spoke of their father, I could literally see the love in their eyes. I remember one occasion when my uncle said, "Our mother could be a difficult woman, but our father was a wonderful man, just a wonderful man." To that my father murmured, "Wonderful man," and there were tears both in my father's and in my uncle's eyes. I thought about how much I had missed in not knowing a man who had inspired such love in his sons. Shortly before my father died at the age of eighty-five, he gave me my grandfather's gold pocket watch. "This is the first thing my dad bought when he came to the United States from Ireland. My mother gave it to me after he died, but I wanted you to have it before I died." Needless to say, I treasure the watch as a connection to the grandfather I never knew.

Fortunately for them, many of the young men at St. X know their grandparents very well, and their grandparents play a very significant role in their lives. In these days of single parent families and of families where both parents have to work, grandparents frequently become the "Rocks of Gibraltar" in a teenage boy's life. Every day I see grandmothers and grandfathers drop students off in the morning and pick them up in the afternoon. When I ask students to write about significant people in their lives, I very frequently get compositions about grandma or grandpa. I remember once a father telling me that he envied the relationship that his son had with his father. When the father said, "I wish that I had the relationship with my own father that my son has, and I wish that I had the relationship with my son that my father has," he was expressing a sentiment which I suspect many fathers share. Of course, grandparents can love unconditionally without having to worry about the day-to-day discipline which parents cannot ignore.

Over the years, I have seen grandparents who have taken over financial responsibility for their grandsons because of problems beyond the family's control. I remember one elderly St. X alumnus who had to assume the care of his grandson when the grandfather was in his sixties. He wanted desperately for the boy to come to St. X, but he couldn't afford it. He came to see Brother Edward, my predecessor, and Brother Edward promised him the boy would go to St. X. When I arrived at

St. X, I kept Brother Edward's promise. To this day, whenever I see the man, he mentions Brother Edward and begins to cry. He was grateful that the Xaverian Brothers had stood by him in his difficulties. I was incredibly impressed that he had taken on the care of a grandson when he could rightfully look forward to a quiet retirement. Imagine dealing with a teenage boy when you are in your seventies!

Grandparents are frequently in evidence at all of Saint Xavier's extracurricular activities. At games, at plays and even on PTA night, grandparents of St. X boys are there to express their love and their concern for the Tigers in their lives. I recall a beautiful scene one afternoon at a tennis match when a senior on the team went over to his grandfather, hugged him and said, "Thanks for coming to watch me play, Grandpa." The grandfather replied, "I wouldn't miss it." You could definitely see love in both their eyes and gratitude on the part of the boy for his grandfather's devotion to him. The boy's father had to work and couldn't make it to an afternoon tennis match, but grandpa could and did.

In an essay which he wrote at the beginning of the school year, one of my students, Justin Walker, had this to say about his grandmother:

> Since my grandma picks me up from school two or three days a week, I am privileged to spend some significant time with her, time that I never fully appreciated. As my grandmother drives, we share the highlights of the day and our plans for the next day. Always learning something new, Grandma talks about the newest report she has seen or the newest article she's read. Every day my grandmother finds something new that she considers fascinating. Last year on the days she drove me

home, she asked me to teach her French and, despite my poor tutelage, she traveled to France that year with a knowledge of the basic language. Grandma was just being herself, a woman able and anxious to expand her horizons.

Justin went on to write about a serious health problem which faced his grandmother and how seriously her problem affected him. Fortunately, she recovered and he became very consciously aware of how very much his grandmother means to him.

As we begin November, the Church celebrates the great Feast of All Saints. In many ways, grandparents are the "living saints' whom God sends into the lives of teenage boys to help them on their road to manhood. Our faith tells us that grandparents who have already gone home to God are still caring and interceding for their children and grandchildren from their place in heaven. I'm sure that, from his place in heaven, my grandfather is keeping an eye on the grandson who bears his name.

Whether they be Grandma and Grandpa or Mamaw and Papaw, may the good Lord bless these grandparents, living and dead, for their untiring love and concern for their grandchildren.

On Sister Miriam Patricia and Cheating

You are perhaps asking yourself, "Where does he get all these stories about old nuns?" Well, I paid very close attention in high school, and I learned far more than math, English and Latin from the nuns. I learned some very good life lessons, and to those women I will be eternally grateful.

Sister Miriam Patricia taught me Latin during my sophomore year of high school. An elderly woman at the time, Sister Miriam Patricia had spent her life teaching chemistry and physics and, as she approached retirement, she taught Latin and German because she found them less taxing. She was not the most energetic teacher at that time in her life, but she knew her stuff, and she pounded Latin grammar into our heads with every trick her fifty years in the classroom had taught her.

On one occasion, we were called to the office to receive our report cards from Sister Adelbert, the Principal. Sister Miriam Patricia told us that she wasn't up to the long trek to the office, so she would remain in the classroom until we returned. When we returned, we discovered fifteen Latin books on her desk and, adolescents that we were, we suspected that we were in for some trouble. We were! Never raising her voice and not seeming the least upset, Sister Miriam Patricia said, "Boys and girls, I have suspected for the last month that some of you have been using prepared translations for your Latin homework rather than doing the work yourself. While you were at the office, I examined your Latin books, and I have on my desk fifteen books which had prepared Latin translations stuffed into the pages. Those of you whose books I have taken will fail Latin for the marking period. You will go to the back of the room, and I will not teach you for the rest of this marking period. You will, however, have to pay attention carefully since Latin is a sequential subject, and you will not be able to pass the next marking period without knowing what I have taught this marking period. Passing off another person's work as your own is cheating, boys and girls, and we don't cheat."

In those pre-Vatican II days when the Church was not terribly ecumenical, we sophomores at Marian High School knew exactly what Sister Miriam Patricia meant by "we." She meant that students in other schools which weren't Catholic might cheat, but we Catholic boys and girls in a Catholic school certainly didn't. Of course, she knew that we had just cheated. Marian High School in the early 1960s was an Irish ghetto. I suspect that 85% of the student body was of Irish descent, and Sister Miriam Patricia was an Irish nun. She was using Irish guilt as a motivator, a tactic which most of our mothers had used on us most of our lives. I can't say that it was ineffective. Probably none of the students who failed Latin that term ever told their parents. To do that, you would have to admit that you cheated. It was far easier to say that you just hadn't studied hard enough and that you would do better next term. Sister Miriam Patricia probably knew that none of us would tell our parents. She didn't tell them either.

As long as there have been schools, schoolboys have cheated. When teenage boys cheat, it has far more to do with laziness than it does with dishonesty. It's far easier to create a "crib sheet" than it is to learn vocabulary words. It's far easier to glance at the paper of the guy sitting next to you than it is to learn those pesky math formulas. It's far easier to download a paper from the Internet than it is to write one. Taking the easy way out is an adolescent strong suit, and some would say that it's a male strong suit. Be that as it may, cheating is something that school teachers and parents cannot overlook. Even if it is motivated by laziness, it is dishonest, and dishonesty is a habit which parents and school teachers have to discourage at all times. While dishonesty during adolescent years might be about trifling things, it can too easily become a moral flaw if it is left unchecked. I think the sad state of our country during the past few months is a warning to all of us about habits of dishonesty.

If you hear from one of your son's teachers that he has been caught cheating, your first instinct will probably be to defend him. Please don't. More likely than not, he is guilty. Cheating is frequently a "teacher's call," and I have found that most teachers have pretty good gut instincts about cheating. I recall one young man years ago whom I suspected of not writing his own essays. His parents protested, and I resolved it by giving him a vocabulary quiz on one of his essays. I assumed that, if he had written the paper, he should certainly know how to spell the words and how to use them in context. He didn't. His father had been "helping him" write his papers. In fact, his father was doing far more than helping. What amazed me at the time was that the father didn't seem to realize that he was putting his son under an incredible handicap for his future education. Where was his son going to learn what he hadn't learned in high school? College? That was a recipe for disaster.

Sister Miriam Patricia has been dead for thirty years, but I learned a lesson from her, and I still use her line. Your sons can tell you that, frequently in my Monday morning fervorinos to the school, I'll say, "We don't do that at St. X." "That" might be any number of things, but I'm not really trying to use Irish guilt. I'm trying to use pride. If the boys at St. X have pride in themselves and pride in the school, then it follows that they will do their work to the best of their ability and that they will be honest with themselves and with others. Honesty and diligence are what we expect from students during their time at St. X. I know that you expect the same of your son. If we teach them honesty and diligence, we are giving them habits for a lifetime.

On Winston Churchill and Parenting

Winston Churchill was one of my father's heroes, and he has become one of mine. I was sorely disappointed when *Time* did not name him Man of the Century. I've read just about everything there is to read about Winston Churchill, from Sir Martin Gilbert's scholarly and magnificent eight-volume biography of Churchill to Norman Rose's less flattering *Churchill, The Unruly Giant* and everything in between. I recently finished the exhaustive *Winston and Clementine: The Personal Letters of the Churchills,* a work edited by their daughter, Lady Mary Soames. When they were apart, Winston and his wife wrote to each other two and three times a day. The book is a remarkable testimony to their love for one another, but as much as I admire them, their letters made me wonder a bit about their parenting skills. Martin Gilbert relates that, toward the end of his life, Churchill had concern for his children:

> There was concern also for the well-being of three of his children; Diana was frequently depressed and sought the help of the Samaritans; Randolph had a fierce temper and lost many friends; Sarah, like Randolph, was a victim of alcoholism, and was hounded by the press. For Churchill, the plight of his

three children, each of whom was talented and affectionate, was a source of pain.[1]

Winston Churchill's own father, Lord Randolph Churchill, was a very distant and very critical father. Like all young Englishmen of his class and era, Winston was sent away quite young to boarding school. He wrote letters to his parents pleading for them to come see him, letters which showed an obvious longing for his father's love and attention. Although his father died quite young, I suspect that much of Winston's life was an attempt to become a man of whom his father could be proud. Unfortunately, because of his own upbringing, Winston was never able to discipline his own son, Randolph, and was certainly overindulgent with him. Randolph managed to alienate most of the people who came in contact with him. There is a story that, when Randolph had a benign tumor removed, one of his contemporaries quipped, "What a shame to remove the one thing from Randolph that isn't malignant." Winston and his son are a fine example of a lack of balance in parenting skills. While Winston obviously desired to love and to rear Randolph in a far better way than his own father had reared him, he apparently went to the opposite extreme. Of course, Randolph had the added difficulty of living in the shadow of a father who had defied Hitler and saved England from destruction. There's not much anyone can do to top that!

Winston and Clementine Churchill came from aristocratic families in a time when it was quite common for parents to entrust their children to the care of nannies and servants. As

1. Gilbert, Sir Martin. *Churchill: A Life*. New York: Henry Holt and Company, 1991: p. 954.

I read the letters of Winston and Clementine, I was amazed at how much time they spent away from their children. While Winston was certainly a workaholic, Clementine seemed to take an inordinate number of vacations to the most exotic of places. Boarding schools and nannies did a great deal to fill in the gaps, although there was a very deep and obvious affection among the Churchill parents and children. Their youngest and sole surviving daughter, Mary, seems to have had the most successful life. She was raised by her nanny, Moppet, who apparently brought stability, love and affection to her life. I wonder if the problems which the Churchill children faced later in their lives had something to do with the time their parents spent away from them. I suspect I am being a bit judgmental here, but still, I have to wonder if their children might have grown up more secure and happier if they had had more of the time and the attention of their parents.

Those of you who have been reading my letters for a period of time will recognize those key words, time and attention. Nothing you can give your children is more important than your time and your attention. My parting advice to the Class of 1999 at graduation last year was this: "As you grow older, remember that nothing should be more important to you than your wife and your children—not your career, not your bank account, not even your golf clubs—nothing!" Over the years, I have had the opportunity to observe many, many families, and the most well-adjusted students I have met come from families where their parents recognize the truth of my graduation advice. Children know instinctively where their parents' values are, and they know instinctively when a career or anything else is more important than they are.

Now, at this point you would certainly be well within your

rights to say, "Fine for you to say, Brother. You don't have to balance a career and children, and you have no wife who needs your regular attention." I would be well rebuked. Nonetheless, I would have to say that I do have a unique perspective on American family life as it pertains to the students at this school. I'll stand by my "time and attention." I've seen nothing else that really works.

I don't normally get discouraged by what I see in modern adolescents. You wouldn't be in this business very long if you did get discouraged because there's more than enough which can be quite discouraging. I may not be discouraged, but I do worry. I worry about how materialistic the students at St. X are and about how much they seem to have received without much effort on their part. The problem is that they come to expect the comforts without the hard work which their parents put into getting those comforts.

The Churchills were able to provide their children with the very best that life had to offer, materially. They lived extraordinary lives, but I am left to wonder if the children would have turned out more well-adjusted if their parents had given them more of their time and their attention and less of the good things life had to offer. Perhaps if Winston had been less indulgent with Randolph, Randolph would have become a more disciplined and friendly man. Perhaps this is all just idle speculation, but in case it isn't, remember time and attention. If you give those two things to your son, he'll know just how important he is to you, and he'll have the security he needs to grow into a mature man and the example he needs to become a good father.

All that being said, I'm still distressed that Churchill wasn't named Man of the Century.

On Dobie the Saint Bernard and Finding the Right Garden

When I was a boy in high school, the school chaplain, Father Shea, had a Saint Bernard named Dobie who spent most of his time sleeping on the cool terrazzo floor outside of Father Shea's office in the senior hallway of the school. While Dobie didn't particularly like the girls in the school, perhaps because they were somewhat afraid of him, he loved the boys because the boys would always stop to pat him on the head or to scratch him behind the ears or to play with him if Dobie were in the mood. Of course, boys and dogs could be the topic of a letter in itself. Dobie was among the most lethargic of very large dogs. On one occasion during my senior year, we had an incredible blizzard; when we returned to school, the snow was piled everywhere and the temperature was frigid. No matter what the weather—rain, sleet or snow—the students at my high school always went out to the school yard after lunch. The boys stood on one side of the school yard and the girls on the other with a nun in the middle watching us like a hawk. When we came out into the school yard on the first day back to school after the blizzard, we were all dumbfounded to find Dobie as frisky as a puppy. He was bounding about the snow banks, barking and having a grand time for himself. The boys, of course, immediately began to play with him, chasing him and throwing snowballs at him. Dobie loved it. Dobie was born and bred to live in the Alps, carrying a cask of whiskey to stranded travelers. By some cruel trick of fate, he found himself in a climate not to his liking. While Massachusetts winters can be cold, they aren't like Switzerland's, and Dobie never seemed to adjust. You might say that Dobie was not in the right garden. He couldn't grow as he was supposed to because he was a mountain dog far from the mountains.

One of your son's tasks as he matures from boy to man is to find the right garden in which to grow, the right climate in which to develop his gifts. The right garden can take a bit of searching, and he may have a number of false starts before he finds it. When we admit a freshman class to St. X, most of the young men take to the school like ducks to water. They have been in the same elementary school for eight years with the same students, and they appreciate the larger environment that St. X has to offer them. It's the right garden at the right time. There are others in the freshman class who take longer to adjust. St. X is the right garden, but it takes them longer to figure that out. Some of them don't figure it out until after they've graduated! There are always a few for whom St. X is just not the right garden. They need either a smaller school or a school that is less "rough and tumble" than the all-male environment of St. X. This search for the right garden goes on during high school and after it. Young people today may attend two or more colleges before they earn a degree and may change their major four or five times. Some do college on the six, seven and even ten-year plan. While this search for the right garden might be frustrating to a young man's parents, hopefully the search will lead him to a productive and happy life. Patience, obviously, is the key for parents with a searching son. Of course, parents have the perfect right to tell the "searcher" after a few years that he has to pay for the search if he plans to continue it over a good number of years.

I think I've probably told this story, but I had a boy in school years ago who was the "classic jock." He had a healthy disdain for anything artistic, and if I had suggested when he was in high school that he would find his life's work in the arts, he would've laughed quite scornfully. Yet, at the tenth reunion of his graduating class from St. John's High, he was an actor, making his way quite successfully in the theater. When I pointed the irony out to him, he shrugged, smiled and said, "Life has a way of changing your perspective, doesn't it?" It took him a while, but he found the right garden in which to grow.

I have a million other examples like him. There was the incredibly lazy and unfocused young man I had in senior English in the late '70s who is now a Ph.D. and a college professor. Then there's my all-time favorite. I had a young man in junior Religion who got his girlfriend pregnant and who had to leave school to marry her. In those days, we wouldn't allow a boy to remain in school if he were married. At his fifteenth reunion he was still with the young lady and had three children. Because his education had been interrupted, he didn't have the best paying job, but I think he was probably the happiest man at that reunion. Fortunately the young lady turned out to be the right woman, and his family provided him with the right garden. He said to me on that night, "A great wife and good kids. What more could a man ask for?" What more, indeed!

You don't want your son to be like Dobie the dog, out of place in his world, wondering what his purpose in life is. His search to find the right garden may take some time, and you may often find it incredibly frustrating. While he's on this search, you'll need patience and understanding and, at times, he'll need a good kick in the butt. You can still give him a good kick and be patient and understanding. That's one of those parental tricks you've learned from experience. When your son is frustrating you because he can't decide where he wants to go to college or what he wants to study, or when he tells you that he needs to go off and ski for a year to find himself, remember Dobie the dog. At some point the weather will turn and, like Dobie, your son will find his garden. Just pray that it happens before he's 30!

On Letting Go

This letter is directed to the parents of the graduating seniors. Parents of underclassmen will have to put this one away until their sons graduate.

My godson, Colin, is the closest thing I'll ever get to a son, and I'm incredibly grateful to his parents for having shared him with me. Colin and I have been very close during his 26 years of life, and whenever I was "back East," I always made a point of getting together with him. We had a godfather/godson tradition of always going to an Irish pub in Worcester, Massachusetts, called O'Connors. Although Colin's name is Novick, his mother's maiden name was O'Malley, so there are good Irish genes mixed in with his Polish genes. I was around for all of the important events in Colin's life, from First Communion through his graduation from the University of Chicago. When he graduated from Chicago, he received an award the week before graduation. His parents couldn't attend, so I stood in for them, thanks to the rather inexpensive airfare from Louisville to Chicago on Southwest Airlines.

Three years ago, Colin called me to tell me that he had just proposed to his girlfriend. Colin has a rather romantic streak to him, so he proposed on the top of Mount Washington. She had the good sense to accept his proposal. The day that he told me of his engagement, I must admit that I had a little twinge. I had to accept that he was growing up and that, with his marriage, there would probably be a significant change in our relationship. When I spoke with his parents after Colin's announcement, I realized that they had some similar feelings. While they were very happy for him because he had found a wonderful woman, they also realized that their son was growing up and that there would be very definite changes in their relationship with him. It was then that I recognized I was having a "parental moment." As I said, Colin is the closest thing I'll ever get to a son, and I was feeling somewhat like a parent must feel in similar circumstances.

On the day of his wedding, I stayed at the Brothers' residence at St. John's High School where Colin's father teaches and where Colin went to school. Colin was very close with one of the elderly Brothers in the community, Brother Philip Neri, and he had invited Brother Philip Neri to his wedding. Unfortunately, Brother Philip Neri's health wouldn't permit his attending the ceremony, but on the day of the wedding, Brother Philip Neri gave me a gift which he had made for Colin and Tracy. Brother Philip was an incredibly talented craftsman. I had always trusted Brother Philip and, as I took the gift from him, I told him that I was having a difficult time with the thought of Colin getting married. I thought that he was a little too young, at the age 22, to be making such a big commitment. Philip Neri replied, "Jimmy, he's not a boy. He's a man, and you have to recognize that. He's certainly old enough to get married, and you should be happy that he's found himself a good woman." I realized immediately the truth of Brother Philip Neri's statement. There was a part of me that didn't want Colin to grow up, but he had grown up, and I had to recognize that.

As your son graduates from St. X and goes on to college

and to life beyond high school, you will probably feel some of the emotional tugs that I felt with Colin. Of course, I didn't have the responsibility of raising him that his parents had. A parent's job is far more difficult than a godparent's job! Parents have a great deal of control over their son's life as he grows up and as they attempt to inculcate in him a proper sense of right and wrong and a good value system.

Even during your son's high school years, you saw the beginning of his drive to independence, which is a natural part of the transition from boy to man. Never underestimate this drive to independence that you will continue to see in your son as he grows older. It's natural and necessary. Realizing that the boy is becoming a man is no easy task for parents. As hard as it is for him to let go of his boyhood and to accept the responsibility of making his own decisions and choices, it is equally difficult for you to relinquish a good bit of the control you once had over his life. It is difficult, too, realizing that his mistakes will be his own and that you will not be able to save him from them. His mistakes will be his own, but so will his triumphs.

Please do not think that I am suggesting that, with his graduation, you lose all say in your son's life. As long as he is living under your roof and you are paying the bills for his tuition and keep, you certainly have a great deal to say about his lifestyle. But he's not a boy anymore and that fact has to be recognized.

I hope that, when your son decides to get married, you'll have the same positive experience that I've had with my godson. I didn't lose a godson; I gained a goddaughter-in-law. Tracy is an English teacher, so we have a lot in common, and I hear from her more frequently than I hear from Colin. I get at least an e-mail a week from Tracy. She has also taken over the task of writing thank-you notes, a task at which Colin never excelled (not that his mother didn't try to inculcate the practice in him as she repeatedly assures me). Now Colin, Tracy, and I go to O'Connors, and I get together with the two of them whenever I'm in Massachusetts. I think that my godson showed remarkable good sense in his choice of a wife, just like his father before him.

On those days when you're having the "parental twinge" as you watch your son grow up, remember that God did not create him to be a boy. He created him to be a man. You didn't raise him to be a boy. You raised him to be a man. You've done that job well, and you can certainly rejoice in a job well done.

On Athletics and Perspective

I stand very frequently on the sidelines at soccer matches, and when Rick Blair was the head coach, I was always intrigued at how nervous this incredibly calm man got when he was coaching. Probably to his chagrin, I would frequently say, “Rick, remember that this is a bunch of school boys playing a game. It’s not the beginning or the end of the world.” He would humor me, but I don’t think that my comments calmed him down at all. Over the years, I have been told by friends that I am overly competitive. Although I am not by any stretch of the imagination an athlete, I like to win and I like to see St. X win. State championships and winning teams are good for the school’s reputation and certainly help our recruitment efforts as well as our alumni fund-raising. That is simply the reality of an all-male institution. Dr. Sangalli and I, however, do try very diligently to let our coaches know that they are not under pressure from us to win at all costs. Quite frankly, I would rather see a St. X team lose in a contest where St. X athletes were not playing fairly or in a gentlemanly fashion. If we have to stretch the rules to win, it’s certainly a hollow victory and one of which we can’t be proud. At St. X, we always want to be proud.

Recently, I have become aware that our coaches are under a great deal of pressure from parents to win and, if I, as head of the school, have to keep perspective on athletics, then I think I can tell you that, as parents, you need to keep the same perspective. Those of you who have sons who are athletes have devoted a great deal of time and energy to your son's athletic career. You have spent hours at soccer camps, football camps and tennis camps. You have invested time and money in your son's athletic talent. That investment of time and money can skew your view of your son and his athletic career. I realize I'm treading on very thin ice here when I say that fathers can lose perspective very quickly, particularly if fathers have coached their sons. But mothers who have been watching junior play sports since he was three years old are not very far behind. In fact, the first time I ever heard a woman use "the f-word" was when I was a young Brother teaching at St. John's High School in Massachusetts. I was standing next to her at a hockey game when she lit into the referee over a call he had made on her son. When I recounted the incident to one of the older Brothers, he simply shrugged and said, "Hockey parents."

I estimate that, in fifteen years as the head of a school, I have signed close to 4,000 diplomas. In those fifteen years and in those 4,000 diplomas, there are only two men who have gone on to play in the major leagues: Jeff Bagwell from Xavier High School in Connecticut and Matt Anderson from St. X. While I recognize that St. X has contributed to major league athletics significantly over the years, the percentage is still minute compared to the number of men who have graduated from the school. The chances of your son becoming a major league player are slim. There is the old issue of college scholarships, and it seems to me that every year St. X graduates win more than their fair share of college athletic scholarships. It's my general impression that many of our athletes who would not be considered stars at St. X have gotten good college scholarship money over the years. They may not play for a Division I school, but they go to respectable schools and play respectable college athletics.

I had a young man in school a few years ago who was on our soccer team. I used to joke with him before a game and ask, "Ryan, how many goals ahead do we have to be before you get into the game?" He would laugh and reply, "At least five!" During his senior year, he told me that it was down to two. We won a state championship in soccer during his senior year, and he was one of the players in the sudden death shoot-out which won the game. His shot eluded the goal-keeper and helped us to win. I think I was as proud of him at that moment as his parents were, so you see I do have some personal investment in the success of St. X athletes. That young man went on to get a good scholarship at a good college, even though he was probably not one of our stars.

As we begin this school year, I want to win as many athletic contests as we can. I would like to win a few state championships and, of course, I would like to beat a certain school on Shelbyville Road in our epic, annual contest. When I feel my overly competitive nature kick in, I need to remind myself that I, as President of the school, need to keep athletics in perspective. As long as St. X athletes are well-coached and taught to play fairly and with class, I can't ask for more from our coaching staff. We are very fortunate at St. X that all of our head coaches are teachers on the faculty. They know the values of the school, and they know that their job is to be good teachers first and good coaches second. In a school of St. Xavier's caliber, academics always trump athletics, and religious and moral development trumps them both. Dr. Sangalli and I have complete confidence in our coaching staff. These are competent men and women who know what we are about as a school.

Two years ago, I was standing next to Rick Blair on a rainy night watching a particularly aggressive soccer game when I saw one of our players slide into the mud. Very deliberately, a member of the opposing team kicked him when he was down. The referee didn't see it. It was all very sneakily done. I went ballistic on the sidelines, and I'm afraid that my language degenerated seriously. At that point, Rick Blair put his arm around my shoulder and said, "Brother, I would like to remind you that it's just a bunch of school boys playing a game." Even the President can lose perspective! I recovered quickly, however, and said, "And if I ever thought that one of our players acted like that and you didn't remove him immediately from the game, you'd be in my office the next morning." To that, Rick Blair replied, "As well I should be."

Let's pray for St. X victories during this coming school year, but let's all keep athletics in its proper perspective. When all is said and done, it really is just a bunch of school boys playing a game.

On Teenage Boys and the Things That Don't Change

> Adolescents are self-indulging, greedy . . . often volatile and contradictory, changing from one moment to the next, quickly tiring of the old and ready for anything new . . . totally impractical, unwilling to listen to advice . . . easily deceived, malleable as wax.
>
> Cardinal Silvio Antoniano (14th Century)

One of the benefits of all the traveling I do is the accumulation of Frequent Flyer Miles. Every summer, my good friend Brother Raymond and I go someplace exotic on my Frequent Flyer Miles. This past summer, we spent two weeks traveling through the Highlands of Scotland. One evening, we were out for a walk in a beautiful Scottish village when we came upon a group of teenagers. They appeared to be waiting for the bus, and the boys in the group were being incredibly obnoxious, obviously showing off for the young ladies in the group. After we passed them, I asked Brother Raymond, "Do you ever just get tired of teenagers?" He replied, "Oh, yes! Particularly when you see behavior that you've seen 10,000 times before, and you know you're going to see 10,000 times again. Even though you know that they're going to outgrow it, it does get a little wearying." As school teachers, we see the stages of adolescent development over and over and, while we do see most of our charges growing through those stages and maturing, it can get a little tiring when, year in and year out, you're dealing with teenage boys going through the more difficult stages of adolescence. I suspect you know what I'm talking about. When you and I are dealing with those difficult periods in your son's adolescence, we need to keep our eyes on the goal and remind ourselves that these stages will pass.

The period of adolescence which I find most difficult to deal with is what I call the "sophomore season of adolescence." I call it that because it hovers around the sophomore year, although it can begin as early as January in the freshman year and, in a worst case scenario, can extend into the senior year. Usually, it begins to pass by January of the junior year. You will know that your son is in "the sophomore season of adolescence" if you find him more than usually difficult to deal with. A father once pinpointed the season for me quite accurately when he said, "Although I love my son very much, I don't particularly like him at the moment." If you don't like your son at the moment, he's probably in this season of adolescence. It's the surly, "know it all" stage of adolescence when your son knows everything, and you know nothing. Your attempts at reason go nowhere because he has a polite (and sometimes not so polite) contempt for your knowledge and experience. He knows it all, and you, out of touch with modern reality as you are, know nothing. Winston Churchill once said that, when he was eighteen, he was amazed at how ignorant his parents were. By the time he turned twenty-one, he was amazed at how much they had learned in three years. I think Winston had a late sophomore season.

This season of adolescence is a time of raging hormones and a desire for independence which your son's economic situation prevents him from realizing. During this time of his adolescence, he'll tell you that all he wants is to get as far away from Louisville, Kentucky, as he can get when he graduates from St. X. A nice college in the Pacific Northwest would suit him perfectly. It's amazing how much of this wanderlust actually cools by graduation. Indiana, Ohio and Tennessee become far enough away for those who actually do go away to school. By that time, Mom and Dad aren't as bad as they seemed a couple of years ago, and his home is not a prison.

A few years ago, I taught a junior class which included a number of young men who were still working through their sophomore season. One of them made it quite clear that he thought I didn't know what I was doing as a teacher. Since I don't take kindly to any guff from my students, he and I had a very bumpy beginning of the year. At PTA, his mother told me that she thought that part of the problem was that the boy's father and I were very similar in temperament. She didn't state this as a criticism, but as a matter of fact. Around January of that year, I noticed that the young man and I were getting along much better and, by the end of the year, we actually seemed to like each other. Just before school began this year, the young man, now a sophomore in college, stopped in to visit and we had a wonderful, very adult conversation. He shared with me some poetry which he had written, much of which I liked very much. After he left, I reflected a bit on my conversation with Brother Raymond in Scotland. Yes, I do get tired of teenagers occasionally, but I do know that it is the rare one who doesn't ultimately grow up and become a responsible and reasonable adult.

If you find your son in the sophomore season of adolescence, you have to muster every bit of energy you have to make sure that he doesn't wear you down. Keep your eye on the goal! This season of adolescence will pass, and he'll become a lovable, and even likeable, young man once again, reasonable and fairly easy to deal with. Once the sophomore season of adolescence starts, however, it just has to run its course, and you have to let him know that there are lines that you are not going to let him cross. Make it clear that he is not to speak to you in a rude and surly manner, and, as long as you are paying the bills, he is not going to call the shots at home. Remember one of Kelly's primary rules for dealing with teenage boys: Say what you mean, and mean what you say. Make no idle threats that you can't or won't keep. Set firm, but reasonable, expectations for your son and stick to them. If he knows that you are going to back down the minute he starts to give you grief, then you'll have no end of grief. If he learns that you are not going to budge, then he'll probably come grudgingly into line.

We adults can forget just how difficult our own adolescence was. While your son may not be a joy to you now, you were perhaps not a joy to your own parents when you were the age that your son is now. I know I wasn't. Pray for patience, and trust that, with God's grace, the season will pass and that God will count the grey hairs your son has given you during this season toward your eternal salvation.

On Training Puppies

I live with Brother Giles, our freshman counselor. The other night at dinner, he mentioned that he'd been getting a lot of complaints about name-calling among the freshmen, and he suggested that I should perhaps say something again during my Monday morning pep talk. Of course, both Dr. Sangalli and I have addressed this issue numerous times with the student body, but I gave it one more crack the next Monday morning. When I finished, Dr. Sangalli said, "It's just boys, you know. We're not going to change their nature." I am quite well aware of that. They call each other names. They push. They shove. They fight, and unfortunately, they can even cheat and steal. It's all what I refer to as "the nature of the beast." Boys are natural experimenters. They are always testing limits, and they will push those limits as far as they can until someone calls them up short. Most of the time, the limits being tested involve fairly childish nonsense, but when it comes to drugs, alcohol, sex, and driving, the limits being tested can have some serious consequences. Dr. Sangalli and I have addressed the issue of alcohol abuse often in our monthly letters.

Obviously, we cannot tolerate unacceptable behavior on the part of the young men in this fine school. The recent rash of school violence in the United States puts things like name-calling and bullying in a whole new context. Although we have never tolerated such behavior at St. X, we find ourselves, as a school, being far more aggressive about confronting this type of behavior. When the boys cross the line, we land on them, sometimes gently, sometimes aggressively, but always very clearly. Boys always need to know very clearly what the consequences of crossing the line are. Let me tell you a couple of stories to illustrate my point.

The other day I was wandering about the school to see what was going on, and I visited Herr Knoop's German class. On the wall of the classroom, Herr Knoop has the "Fabulous Five" for each of his classes. The "Fabulous Five" are the top five boys in each class. In the class I was visiting, there was a young man whom I had recently taken to task for some rather childish behavior in another class; lo and behold, he was listed on Herr Knoop's wall as one of the "Fabulous Five" for his class. I looked at the young man. He smiled. "Let me explain this to you, son. You're on the 'Fabulous Five' here in Herr Knoop's class because you know that Herr Knoop won't tolerate the slightest bit of nonsense from you and that he expects you to do your work and to do it well. Isn't that right?" The young man smiled again. He said nothing, but I knew how to interpret the smile. The smile said, "Well, of course. What else did you expect?" This reminded me of a student focus group I had attended a few weeks before when some juniors and seniors commented that there are a few teachers at St. X who tolerate more than they should from students and that the students would come into line very quickly if those teachers made it clear where the line was. As head of the school, I found that a very interesting reflection on the part of students.

A few weeks ago, I took to task one young man in my class because he had not followed instructions which I had given very clearly and which I had even put into writing. When he came to me after school with the work done according to the original specifications, I told him I was sorry I had taken him on, but that I expect my students to listen to instructions and to do what I tell them. He shrugged and said, "That's OK, Brother. My dad's taken me on a lot worse than that." He made that remark with a smile suggesting that taking him on was one of his dad's jobs. He just expected it.

If you'll pardon the analogy, raising a teenage boy is very much like training a puppy. When a puppy creates a mess, you rap him on the nose with rolled up newspaper to get his attention and to help him learn limits. Occasionally, you have to rub his nose in the mess he's made to make sure that he gets the point. If you train your puppy well, when he grows into his feet and becomes a mature dog, he will know the limits almost instinctively, and he'll know the lines he's not supposed to cross. Puppies can be somewhat exasperating to train because they have a lot of puppy energy which they have a hard time containing. As with puppies, so with teenage boys. They need, occasionally, to have their noses rubbed in the messes they've made, and they frequently need to be rapped on the nose, figuratively speaking, with a rolled up newspaper. Nine times out of ten, it's their excessive energy which gets them into the most trouble. And just like puppies, boys eventually grow into their feet.

Neither you nor I are going to change the nature of the beast. Boys will always be boys, and they will only learn to become men if we teach them their limits and the lines they are not to cross. It can be a very frustrating task, but also a very rewarding task. Finally, to finish my puppy analogy, you can rap a puppy on the nose and he'll come back moments later wagging his tail. Like puppies, boys don't hold grudges. It's one of the nice things about puppies, and it is certainly one of the nicest things about boys.

On Being Careful With Our Words

His parents used to go every year for the Feast of the Passover, and when He was twelve they went up for the celebration as was their custom. As they were returning at the end of the feast, the child Jesus remained behind unknown to His parents. Thinking He was in the party, they continued their journey for a day, looking for Him among their relatives and acquaintances. Not finding Him, they returned to Jerusalem in search of Him. On the third day they came upon Him in the Temple sitting in the midst of the teachers, listening to them and asking them questions. All who heard Him were amazed at His intelligence and His answers. When His parents saw Him they were astonished, and His mother said to Him: "Son, why have you done this to us? You see that your father and I have been searching for you in sorrow." He said to them: "Why did you search for me? Did you not know that I had to be in my Father's house?" But they did not grasp what He said to them. He went down with them then, and came to Nazareth, and was obedient to them. His mother meanwhile kept all these things in her heart. Jesus for His part progressed steadily in wisdom and age and grace before God and men.

LUKE 2: 41–52

Not long ago, I witnessed a rather disturbing scene between a mother and a daughter in an airport. The daughter was perhaps eleven or twelve years old, and she and her mother had been traveling together. Apparently, the daughter had not been a joy on this particular trip, and Mom was not happy. At one point, the mother turned to her daughter and said, "Mary, I am so over you." Now, I realize that "I'm so over you" is almost a cliché, but I was appalled that a mother would say that to her child. Before I became too judgmental, however, I realized that there have been many times in my career when I've said things to students that I wish I hadn't. That's the problem with teenagers. They can drive us adults into some very childish behavior. I recall once, 20 years ago, being very angry with a senior in my English class. In my frustration, I told him that he was a loser. To this day, I remember the look of hurt on his face. Even 20 years later it haunts me. I can't honestly remember how I reacted to that look. I hope that I had enough sense to calm down and apologize, but even if I did that, once you have said a word, it can't be taken back. I still pray for that kid, and I hope that his memory of his Catholic education and his senior English teacher are not totally clouded by his teacher's frustration on that day.

At the beginning of every school year, I tell our "rookie" teachers that they always have to remember that, in any interaction with a St. X student, they are the adult. Kids will act like kids because they aren't adults. Teenagers can say some very hurtful things to their parents, to their teachers and even to their friends, and we adults have to forgive them because they are kids and, therefore, frequently lack maturity. Of course, the older they grow, the more responsible we hold them. There are things at St. X that we might tolerate from a 14-year-old freshman that we certainly wouldn't tolerate from an 18-year-old senior. But even seniors can lack judgment and say things that can be hurtful to the adults in their lives. We adults, however, just don't have that luxury when we're dealing with teenagers. We adults can't act like kids because we aren't kids. We have the awesome responsibility of being role models.

I suspect that, over the last fourteen to eighteen years, there have been times when you have said things to your son which you wish you hadn't said, things which, as soon as they were out of your mouth, you regretted. Your son may say things at times which hurt you to the quick, but it's always best not to respond in kind. The devastating retort might be on the tip of your tongue, but remember that he's the kid and you're the adult. There are times when you have to take your son to task, and take him to task quite vigorously. Even as you do that, watch your words. Let the tone of your voice do the trick and not your vocabulary.

Theologians tell us that, in the Gospel scene which serves as the epigraph of this letter, Jesus is beginning to understand his special relationship with God. From a theological point of view, I'm sure they are probably right. I have never read this gospel story without thinking that it is a perfect example of the Catholic belief that Jesus was fully human and fully divine. In this story, He certainly shows himself as a very human early adolescent. Theologians posit that Jesus is showing great insight into His divine nature. I think that He's being a smart-alecky, know-it-all adolescent. I'm sure that the part of this scene that the gospel writer chose *not* to record is St. Joseph saying, "We'll have no more smart mouth out of you, young man, and you'll watch your tone of voice when you speak to your mother." Mary probably had a talk with Jesus later about hurting St. Joseph's feelings: "Yes, dear, I know that God is your father, but whose work is it that puts food on our table every night and clothes on our backs? He's your father, too." Jesus was probably a typical teenager, but Mary and Joseph probably handled him pretty well, watching their words carefully. They must have been doing something right because, as the gospel writer tells us, Jesus was obedient to them and grew in wisdom, age, and grace.

Your sons can confirm that I'm not a man who lets teenagers get away with much, and my temper can get the better of me on occasion. But since that day 20 years ago when I looked at the incredible hurt in my student's face, I have tried to be cautious with my words. I haven't always succeeded, but I've tried. And I've always had the good sense to apologize when I've failed. When you are not happy with your son, be cautious with your words. When the storm has passed, you'll feel better about how you behaved, and he will have observed positive parenting which he can tuck away in his brain for that day in the distant future when he's angry with his son. And whatever you do, don't squabble with your son in an airport. You never know when there might be a headmaster lurking about, ready to write a letter about you!

On Saying Goodbye

When I first became a principal in 1982, the process was far easier than when I applied to be President of St. X and then President of Mount Saint Joseph. In those long ago days, the appointment of the head of a Xaverian Brothers school was the prerogative of the Provincial Superior and not the Board of Directors. In March of 1982, after a brief interview process, I received a phone call from Brother James Sullivan, the Provincial of the Boston Province of the Xaverian Brothers, informing me that I had been appointed principal of Xavier High School. Since he was my religious Superior, I asked Brother James for a few pious words to encourage me in my new position. He replied, "You're fifteen years younger than the next youngest Brother in charge of one of our schools. Some of my counselors think that you're too young, but I appointed you anyway. Don't screw up or you'll make us both look bad." As you can tell, Brother James Sullivan was a straight-shooter. He never minced words.

During my first term as principal of Xavier, I made a number of notable mistakes, none of them tragic, and Brother James Sullivan was not shy about giving his opinion of those mistakes. He had, however, a remarkable way of taking me to task for what I hadn't done well without making me feel that he had lost confidence in me. In many ways, we had a father-son relationship and, since we were both of Irish extraction, it was as complicated as Irish father-son relationships can get. He reminded me frequently that I was not simply the principal of a 2x4 Catholic high school in the middle of a cow pasture in Middletown, Connecticut. I was also a Xaverian Brother in charge of one of the corporate ministries of the Xaverian Brothers, an awesome responsibility, a sacred task. I was the spiritual father of a school of 800 boys, and I had the responsibility always to give a good example. He got most distressed with me when he thought that I was giving bad example. The ironic thing was that he would frequently chide me for my occasionally salty language when he himself was far saltier than I. He just never got salty in public!

Through seventeen years as the head of two schools, I have tried to be the spiritual father of the school community, and I don't have to tell you that fathers can make mistakes. For those mistakes which I have made during my eight years as President of St. X, I sincerely apologize. As part of my role as spiritual father of the school, I have always considered it one of my prime responsibilities to be a support and encouragement to you, our parents. I've done that primarily through my writing. Over eight years, I have written perhaps 85 letters to parents and, although I've used many different metaphors, it's fairly easy to sum up my main message: Pay attention to your son! Don't let a day go by when you haven't made the bold attempt to talk with him, even if all he does is grunt in reply. Get to know his friends, and always know where he is and what he is up to. In every conceivable way, let him know every day how much you love him and how important he is to you, even on those days when he is being his most unlovable. Keep him on a leash that's loose enough to let him make his own mistakes and tight enough to ensure that those mistakes aren't disastrous.

Pray for your son every day, remembering that God's grace can do miraculous things with your less-than-perfect parenting.

Recently I read an article about Archbishop Tutu of South Africa. In it he commented on the problems he had raising his own son. He said, "The most gorgeous moment (in my life) would be when I became a father for the first time, April 14th, 1956, when our only son, our Trevor, was born. I was so proud and so happy. It made me feel a little like God and, later, with the way Trevor has lived his life, taking the wrong turns and causing pain and anguish, I have learned something of the impotence God feels as he watches his children making the wrong choices. Sometimes, in my own life as a father, I have felt very like God looking at us and thinking, 'Whatever got me to create that lot?' " I was very much struck by the Archbishop's words. You, as parents, and I, as the spiritual parent of this school, have experienced exactly what Archbishop Tutu describes, our feelings of impotence and disappointment when we see our sons and students making poor choices and going in wrong directions. On those occasions, we have to be like the father in the parable of the prodigal son, waiting patiently for the prodigal's return, ever ready to forgive and forget.

When I was a novice Xaverian Brother, my novice master, Brother Kevin, used to tell us that we should never compare schools at which we had been missioned. He would say, "Wherever you're missioned now is the best place you've ever been." There was some real wisdom in that. I've had the good fortune over thirty years to love each of the three schools at which I have been missioned. That has been particularly true for St. X, and leaving this wonderful school is going to be very difficult for me. I read an article recently in the Tennessee Catholic paper by a Dominican nun who wrote, "When, as a religious, you leave a mission, the last thing you pack is your heart, and when you arrive at your new mission, the first thing you unpack is your heart." Rather pious, but true. I'm sure that, however many years from now the time comes for me to leave Mount Saint Joseph, I'll be as sad to leave there as I am now to leave St. X, and that will be a sign, then, as it is now, that I've done my job.

On one occasion at Xavier High School when I had used rather salty language over the public address system, I received a letter from Brother James Sullivan (who, by coincidence, had been in the school on that day), chiding me for my language. The letter was firm, yet fatherly. It closed with, "Well, Jim, I guess you just can't shine a sneaker." My principalship at Xavier outlasted his provincialship. When his term as Provincial ended, he became a member of the Xavier Board. He died very suddenly of a heart attack during his Board term and one of my last interactions with him came after a Board meeting. As he was leaving, he patted me on the back and said, "Nice job. Good boy." Although I was in my forties at the time, I wasn't at all put off by the paternal tone. In fact, I hope that from his place in heaven, he's saying the same thing about my presidency at St. X.

Please know that the St. X community will always be in my prayers. Please keep me and Mount Saint Joseph in yours.

SECTION TWO

MOUNT SAINT JOSEPH

2001–PRESENT

In the fall of 2000, I was happily ensconced at Saint X with every plan of staying there for at least another year. Barry Fitzpatrick was functioning as both the President and the Principal of the Mount, and the Board was looking for a President so that Barry could return to his first love, being the Principal. A number of people, including Barry and the late Brother Lambert, asked me if I would consider coming to the Mount. While the thought of the Mount intrigued me, I was so happy at Saint X that I really didn't want to consider leaving. Then, Brother Lawrence Harvey, the Director of our Sponsored Schools, chimed in with his opinion, and I began to think more seriously about the Mount. The final decision came down to an election! I was running for First Vice-President of the Louisville Rotary. If elected First Vice-President, I would automatically succeed to the presidency in the following year. I had invested a lot of time in the Rotary, and I wasn't prepared to leave Louisville if, in fact, I were elected into the presidential sequence. I said to myself, "If you win, you stay. If you lose, you go to the Mount." I lost! The rest is history. Of course, in hindsight, I can see the wonderful Providence of almighty God at work.

In June of 2001, I left Saint X to drive to the Mount. As I came to the Kentucky/West Virginia border, I drove into a torrential downpour and had to pull off the road into a rest area. The sympathetic fallacy seemed to be at work. The weather reflected my mood. I sat in that rest area for forty-five minutes and added not a few tears to the rain pouring around me. When the skies cleared, I drove on to Baltimore. At the time of the publication of this book, I have spent ten incredibly happy years at Mount Saint Joseph. Mount boys won my heart from the beginning. They are "Israelites in whom there is no guile," young men without airs or pretensions. And they are the friendliest teenage boys I have ever met!

On the Ingredients of Good Parenting

When I was leaving Saint Xavier in Louisville, the MOMS Club asked me to devise a recipe for good parenting which they could use as the introduction to the cookbook they were publishing. I was at Mount Saint Joseph for six months before I finally honored their request. I think that I got the document to them moments before it was to be published! I thought you might enjoy reading the recipe that I sent to the Saint X mothers:

An ABILITY to speak to him respectfully, even when he isn't being respectful.

INSIGHT to help him see that sometimes his failures are more important than his successes.

COURAGE . . .

. . . to bring him back into line when he is out of line;

. . . to stick to your guns when you know that what he wants is not what he needs.

KNOWLEDGE that "like and love" are not the same thing.

TIME and ATTENTION, even when he seems to be telling you that he doesn't want your time or attention.

PATIENCE with his fumbling attempts at becoming a man and his, at times, impulsive words and actions.

FORGIVENESS for the times he hurts you when he isn't even aware that he has.

UNDERSTANDING that he really does love you, even when he hurts you.

REALIZATION that boys grow much more quickly physically than they do emotionally and spiritually.

VIGILANCE—so that you can anticipate problems before they become too serious.

A HEART that hears all that isn't said.

LOVE that is unconditional, but knows when to be tough.

WISDOM that knows when it is best to let him make his own mistakes and when it is best not to.

HUMILITY . . .

. . . that understands your limitations as a parent, but also understands the power of God's grace;

. . . that is willing to apologize to him when you're wrong.

WILLINGNESS to let him go when he is ready to fly on his own.

RESPECT for the man that he is in the process of becoming, even as you support the boy he still is.

You might perhaps wonder why you should heed the advice of a childless celibate about parenting, but, as I always tell you, parenting and teaching are kissing cousins. They require the same skills. Oh, and finally, as you stir all of these ingredients together, always remember Saint Benedict's advice to his monks, and "listen with the ear of your heart."

On Telling the Truth

In the seventeen years that I have been the head of a school, I have had to deal fourteen times with the death of a student during the school year. The very fact that I can remember the exact number gives you some indication of how traumatic such a death is for a school community. On these sad occasions, I consider it my primary responsibility to support the parents as best I can and to put the death within the context of our faith for the student body. Death is an incredible affront to adolescents. They feel that they are immortal, and the death of a classmate shatters, for a brief moment, that illusion. I say for a brief moment because teenagers can put the death of a classmate out of their mind very quickly. It's their way of coping with something they can't possibly understand. During my career, I have given many eulogies for boys who did not live to be men. Since I realize that there is nothing I can say to parents which will assuage their grief, I can only offer the support and the presence of the school community. For the students, I can attempt to give the context of our faith, even though I know they might not be ready to hear it.

During my last year as Principal in Connecticut, a young man was killed tragically in a car wreck which was by no means his fault. I did my best to support the parents, and I gave the eulogy at his funeral. Since his mother was a teacher in the local public school system, the Superintendent of Schools also spoke at the funeral, offering the sympathy of the school district and of her colleagues. As the two of us walked out of church together after the final commendation, he began to talk. Surprisingly, this public school superintendent reminded me of the great privilege that I have as a Catholic educator. He said:

> I'm so jealous of you. I get to stand before the congregation and offer sympathy to the parents. You get to stand before the congregation and tell them the truth. I say that I'm sorry their son is dead. You get to remind them that he's not dead and that they will, indeed, see him again. You have the privilege of telling them the truths of our faith and, because I'm in public education, I don't. I'm a devout Catholic, and it's always bothered me that I can never publicly tell anyone what I believe. How wonderful it is that you can. I get to offer sympathy. You get to tell the truth.

I was rather taken aback by these comments because I take so for granted the fact that I get to speak and to teach within the context of faith. I've never taught in anything but a Catholic school, so faith is the context in which I have spent my entire career in education. I've never been in a school situation where I couldn't express my beliefs and celebrate the truths of our faith. It took a public school superintendent to remind me what a privilege I have.

I once had a student remind me of this privilege in a rather unusual circumstance. I was still teaching full-time, so it had to be before 1980. I was prefecting College Board exams on a Saturday at Xavier High School. The students taking the exam were largely boys from Xavier and girls from Mercy

High School, but there were a number of students, perhaps four or five, from the public high school. As I was about to begin the exam, one Xavier boy said, "Aren't we going to pray? We always pray before everything. We should certainly pray before this test." I explained to him that, since there were students from the public school in the room, we couldn't force our belief on them. He was not satisfied. He turned to the kids from the public school who were sitting in the back of the room and said, "You guys don't mind if we pray, do you?" The public school students looked rather uncomfortable and said nothing. The Xavier boy took that as assent and said to me, "They don't mind. Pray!" We prayed. Praying before that exam may have had something to do with superstition on the boy's part, but it also might have been a reflection of the context in which he had been educated. He knew that "we always pray before everything." The school always operated within the context of faith, and he had learned that lesson. Last year, I had dinner with a former student of mine who is a doctor. I had taught him freshman religion eighteen years ago. We were in a restaurant and, when the waitress brought dinner, he looked at me and said, "Aren't we going to say grace?" I have never prayed in restaurants, but the question certainly did my teacher's heart good. I suspect that his desire to say grace had far more to do with his upbringing than my teaching, but nevertheless, his question did remind me of the privilege of educating in faith.

We are about to celebrate the great mysteries of our faith, the passion, death and resurrection of our Lord. We Catholics are a sacramental church, and there is nothing more beautiful than the liturgy of Holy Week when we celebrate sacramentally the truths of our faith. At the Easter Vigil, the Church reminds us quite forcefully that death doesn't have the last word. Christ does.

The public school superintendent told me that he hoped, when he retired from the public school system, to teach in a Catholic school so that he would get "to tell the truth." I don't know if that ever happened, but I do know that he was an occasion of grace for me. He reminded me of the wonderful privilege I have to be able to teach within the context of faith. That faith reminds us during the Easter Season that Christ is Risen and that death doesn't have the last word. We have everything to hope for and nothing to fear.

Happy Easter!

On Mixed Signals

To keep myself in touch with Kentucky, I still subscribe to one of the weekly Louisville papers. In last week's issue, there was a beautiful action photo of a Saint X basketball game on the front page. One of my former students was taking a jump shot which the photographer captured beautifully. That photo brought back many warm memories of the student and of my years at Saint X.

I recall sitting next to that boy's father at a basketball game last year. I told him what a fine young man his son was and how much I enjoyed teaching him. He thanked me, but, like all fathers, he seemed somewhat embarrassed at having his son praised to his face. After a few minutes of silence, he said, "You know, Brother, I'm a Saint X grad, but when I was here, I didn't do very much and I certainly wasn't an athlete. I am actually enjoying my son's time at Saint X more than I enjoyed my own. I think it's just great that I can come and watch him play ball. I never miss one of his football games or his basketball games, never. I have been so blessed in my children." You could actually hear the love for his son in his voice, and I thought to myself, "No wonder Connor is such a good kid. He has parents who love him and who pay attention to him."

No matter how long I stay at Mount Saint Joseph or how many letters I write to you, there is one theme you will read repeatedly: time and attention. Your son needs your time and your attention. I think that if there is a recipe for good parenting, time and attention are two of the key ingredients. Now, your son will lead you to believe that he doesn't want your time or your attention. He will lead you to believe that all that he wants is for you to leave him alone. Believe me when I tell you that leaving him alone is the last thing he really wants and the last thing that he really needs. Being a boy, he can't express it to you. Boys have a hard time articulating whatever they feel deeply, and they can give some very mixed signals. When you are trying to pay attention to your son and he says, "Get off my case," what he is really saying is, "Please stay on my case because, if you do that, I'll know that you love me." It's all very confusing, but believe me—it's true. As your son gets into the upper grades in high school, it can be hard to keep track of him, but it is important that you do and that you continue to give him your time and attention.

A few years ago, after a school play, I discovered a senior in an empty hallway behind the auditorium crying his eyes out. He wasn't a boy who usually expressed much emotion, so I was concerned. When I asked what the problem was, he said, "My parents didn't come to see me perform in the play." I asked him if he had told his parents that he wanted them to come and that the play was important to him. He replied, "They should have known that it was important to me. It's all I've talked about for the last month." Now, I can't judge the boy's parents because I don't know what else was going on in their lives, but I do know that, on that night, they had a broken-hearted son and a lost opportunity. Again, part of the problem is teenage communication. He probably couldn't bring himself to say to his parents, "I really want you to come to the play. It's important to me." Unfortunately, boys are never that direct.

Give your son your time and your attention and don't worry about any of the grumbling that he does or the seeming attempts to push you away. He can't articulate it now, but years from now, he will be grateful, and he will have learned some good parenting skills for the time when he has a son of his own.

On Humor and Proportion

> Give a boy a sense of humor and a sense of proportion, and he will stand up to anything.
>
> Mr. Chips in the 1939 movie *Goodbye, Mr. Chips*

Over the holidays, I watched one of my favorite movies, *Goodbye, Mr. Chips*. This 1939 classic, based on James Hilton's novel and set in an English boys' boarding school in the last decades of the 19th and early decades of the 20th century, recounts the life of Mr. Chipping, a man who teaches generations of boys at Brookwood School. Since Mr. Chips, in the final years of his career, is the embodiment of Brookwood School, he does not hesitate to challenge the modern ideas of a new headmaster. When the headmaster suggests that Mr. Chips is too old-fashioned to be effective with boys and that his methods don't produce what the headmaster would call success, Mr. Chips replies, "Give a boy a sense of humor and a sense of proportion, and he will stand up to anything." As I watched the movie, the truth of those words struck me quite forcefully.

If one of the purposes of education is to help students find ways to cope with life, then Mr. Chips certainly knew his educational pedagogy. A sense of humor and a sense of proportion are certainly key elements in a well-balanced life, but how does a boy, or anyone for that matter, develop a sense of humor and a sense of proportion? And how can a school assist in developing those qualities?

While you would probably like to see your son sail through life without any difficulties, I am afraid that it is failure which best teaches him a sense of proportion. Teenage boys can think that the world has ended when they fail a test, or when they are cut from a team, or when they are refused by a college, or when one of the lovely young ladies from Mount de Sales or Seton Keough dumps them. When they discover that they can recover from those adversities, they begin to develop a sense of proportion, a sense that not everything in life is equal and that some things are more important than others.

They also learn a sense of proportion by watching the reactions of the adults in their lives to adversity. I watched a mother, at her husband's wake, teach her sons proportion by her reaction to the death of a beloved husband and father. Without words, she said to her sons, "This is just terrible, but we are a family, and we are going to survive it." On a far less serious note, I remember my own father teaching me proportion when, at the age of sixteen, I had my first car accident. He didn't ask me whose fault the accident was until he had ascertained that nobody had been injured. When I told him the accident was my fault, he replied, "Well, we have insurance, and you will probably do far worse than that before you're done." Those words were a significant life lesson for me. They must have been, because I remember them clearly thirty-eight years later. Your son is not going to get through life without experiencing failure. While you can't protect him completely from these things, you can help him to learn a sense of proportion even as you support him in his difficulties.

Now, a sense of humor is a far more difficult topic to discuss.

It seems to me that some people either have a well-developed sense of humor, or they don't. Some people take life so seriously that they are never able to see the humor in anything, while other people see humor everywhere. Whether it is learned or inherited behavior, I don't know. I do know, however, that you can help teenage boys learn to laugh at themselves by laughing at yourself in some of those rather ridiculous situations with which life confronts us. I once gave what I thought was a stirring address to the faculty at Xavier High School in Connecticut, only to have a teacher tell me when I had finished that I needed to blow my nose. It wasn't my stirring words which were causing the faculty's smiles during the speech. I blew my nose and then laughed myself silly. So much for the dignified principal commanding the rapt attention of the faculty! If you and I can learn to laugh at ourselves, then our sons and our students can learn from us. Many years ago, one of our Brothers fell flat on his face, literally, on the first day of school, in front of a sophomore geometry class. He picked himself up, dusted himself off and said, "Well, boys, so much for charm school." He may have taught them a more important lesson by that quip than by all the geometry he taught them during the rest of the school year.

The kids I worry most about are those kids who take themselves too seriously and who are thrown completely by the bumps and bruises of life. They think everything is a disaster. Now, you may more often worry that your son isn't taking life seriously enough. Believe me—that's an easier worry. "Give a boy a sense of humor and a sense of proportion, and he will stand up to anything." You can learn a lot from an old movie!

On Nice Boys and Laziness

When the first marking period was coming to an end, the Studies Office put out a list of coded comments to select from for report cards. I immediately went to Mr. Dave Norton, the Director of Studies, to complain that the most important comments were missing from the list. He asked which comments they might be. I told him that we needed "nice boy, but as lazy as sin" and its companion comment "smart boy, but as lazy as sin." Mr. Norton said that he would look into it. I suspect that many parents would be startled to see such comments on their son's report card, but surprised as they might be, they probably would shake their heads in agreement.

Recently, I was chatting with a junior who told me about his very good SAT scores. Knowing the boy, I commented, "So, you're a smart boy, but you're as lazy as sin." He gave me that cock-eyed look that boys give you when they are not sure if you are kidding. I asked him if he had heard those sentiments expressed before about his ability and his performance. He replied, "Oh, about a thousand times from my parents."

When I first began teaching, my mentor, Brother Ivan, 50 years a Brother and a magnificent teacher, once chided me, "Jimmy, don't yell so much. The boys aren't going to study any harder because you yell at them." I complained to him that I didn't feel that my students were studying as hard as they should. To that he replied, "Boys never study as hard as they should. They have too many more interesting things to do than study. You have to learn how to coax and cajole them into studying. Yelling won't do it." I have come to learn, over 30 years, how very right Brother Ivan was. Even the brightest boys are not natural students. There are just too many more interesting things to do than study. Teenage boys mature physically very quickly, but they mature emotionally, intellectually and spiritually far less quickly. It takes a while for their minds to catch up with their bodies! That time lag can be a real trial to parents and schoolteachers.

While Brother Ivan was right that yelling doesn't help, you might be driven to it when the coaxing and cajoling doesn't seem to be wearing him down. The problem is that, while teenage boys mature emotionally and intellectually rather slowly, you, as a parent, can never let up. You can't simply say, "Well, he's just going to be slow developing emotionally and intellectually, so I am just not going to worry about it." Believe it or not, your son expects you to nag him about studying and about doing the things that he knows he is supposed to do. He'd be surprised if you didn't nag him. You never know when the stars will converge and your son will experience that magic moment when he begins to understand in a very real way that he has incredible potential. Until that day arrives, however, you should never cease, out of frustration or exhaustion, to ask him if his homework is done or if he has all of the books and supplies he needs for school that day or if he has taken the extra time to pound those last few vocabulary words or chemistry formulas into his head.

A mother once complained to me that she felt terrible because she was always nagging her son to get his schoolwork done and to get his act together. I told her that she was his mother, and that was her job. Sons expect that. When I was a senior in high school, I told my mother one day that I wasn't feeling well and that I didn't want to go to school. She said, "Go to school. If you're sick, the nuns will send you home." I was sent home at noon with German measles. Feeling vindicated, I said to my mother, "I told you I was sick." She replied, "And I told you that if you were sick, the nuns would send you home." I shrugged and went to bed. I doubt that my mother gave it another thought. In my adolescent mind, Ma was just being Ma. I think I would have been surprised if she had let me stay home from school. It was my father, however, who chained me to the dining room table every day after school to do my homework when I was going through my "smart boy, but as lazy as sin" period. "Lazy" wasn't in my father's vocabulary.

If your son is "a nice boy or a smart boy, but as lazy as sin," don't worry too much about it. Don't, however, let up on him. After 30 years of batting out fungoes to wondering schoolboys, I can tell you that I have seen legions of nice, but lazy, boys who have become incredibly productive and hard working men. It just takes time. . . . and a good bit of parental nagging!

On Appearance and Reality

Thirty years of working with teenage boys has given me a great deal of insight into the nature of the male adolescent, but there are times when I forget those insights. One such insight which occasionally slips my mind is that the old adage, "You can't judge a book by its cover," is never as true as when it is applied to a teenage boy. You simply can't judge a teenage boy by the way he looks or even by the way he occasionally acts. I was reminded of this very clearly during the last school year.

I was wandering around the cafeteria at Saint X when I came upon Sean, one of the scruffiest members of the senior class. I immediately launched into my school President mode, "Sean, shave and get a haircut. Tuck your shirt in. Put your tie up." He grudgingly complied with the tie and the shirt and promised me that he would shave and get a haircut. It was one of those quick interactions that school administrators have three hundred times a day and to which you don't give much thought after it's over.

Later, in that same lunch period, I wandered out behind the cafeteria where the Dean of Students, Brother Crane, was sneaking a smoke with the cafeteria ladies. There, sitting on a bench, was Joe, a senior who was having incredible emotional problems, and next to him was my friend, Sean. When I called Brother Crane aside and asked him what was going on, he replied that Sean, recognizing that Joe was having incredible problems, came out every day after eating his lunch to sit with Joe. They apparently didn't talk, but Sean gave Joe his quiet support. Bells, of course, went off in my head, and I thought to myself, "Kelly, you idiot!" I had made a quick judgment on Sean because of his appearance, but here was a boy, who, while he might fight us on the dress code, had obviously learned the more important lessons of a Catholic education in a Xaverian Brothers' school. Here was a boy who was looking out for a very troubled classmate and who continued to look out for the troubled classmate even when that classmate did not respond.

In my first month at Mount Saint Joseph, I have had similar experiences. I do think the kids need to look neat, and I will correct them on their appearance. I also know, however, that I can't judge them on appearance. Occasionally, I will point out one of our scruffier students and ask Mr. Fitzpatrick, "What's he like?" The response is always, "One of the nicest kids in the school." I've pointed out to Mr. Fitz that he has said that now about half the student body, and if I asked about the other half, he will probably reply in the same way!

You need to get to know your son's friends. You need to know that your son is hanging around with kids who are going to lead him in the right direction. But I would caution you that you can never judge a book by its cover when it comes to teenagers. Your son may bring home a friend who looks like trouble, but there is a good chance, a very good chance, that he could be "one of the nicest kids in the school." Get to know him before you make any judgment because you really can't judge a teenage boy by his appearance. Neither would you want teachers nor other parents judging your son by his appearance because you know, at times, he can probably look pretty scruffy.

Three days before graduation last year, the Assistant Dean of Students brought Sean to me because he had been told to get a haircut for graduation. He did get a haircut, but he didn't get much cut off. The Assistant Dean wanted a ruling from me as to whether Sean needed a more drastic haircut. While he didn't meet the letter of the law, I approved the haircut, much to Sean's and the Assistant Dean's surprise. How could I quibble about his hair when he had so clearly learned the deeper lessons that the school had to teach? When Sean shook my hand at graduation after he received his diploma, he gave me a big smile, and I returned it, quite proud that this rather scruffy young man represented his alma mater so very well.

On Adolescent Time Schedules

I'll never forget Mrs. Salafia, whose son I taught during his junior year at Xavier High School. She arrived at PTA rather distraught over her son's immaturity. "I have nightmares that I'm going to have a forty-year-old teenager on my hands, still living in my house." I wasn't much consolation since I was fairly young at the time and didn't have much experience. I thought her son was rather immature myself; the week before, he had hidden in the classroom closet at the beginning of class, knowing that the first thing I always did after the start of class was to go to the closet for the daily handouts. When I opened the door, he jumped out, scaring me to death in front of a class of forty juniors.

With age and experience, I have come to learn that teenage boys grow up according to their own schedule, not the schedule of their parents and their teachers. I realized this rather concretely two years ago when I taught a mixed grade class in Latin II. The class was rather small, only seven students, one senior, two juniors and four sophomores. I have always liked teaching juniors because I find them very reasonable and because they don't normally go into a slump at the end of the year as seniors have a tendency to do. Sophomores, on the other hand, can be a tad unreasonable as they go through their growth period, both physically and emotionally. The senior in the class I had taught in English during his junior year, and he was an impeccable student and a superb young man. My Latin was very rusty since I hadn't taught it in fifteen years, and Parker was my life support. Whenever an irregular Latin verb went out of my head, I simply looked at Parker who compensated for my memory lapse. At the beginning of the school year, the juniors were a bit antsy and not terribly sure that they wanted to do the work required of a rather difficult language, but as the weeks went on, they both began to experience some success, and they both began to realize that, with hard work, they had the potential to be very good students. By the end of the year, they were magnificent and quite proud of themselves for all that they had accomplished. At the beginning of the year, the sophomores weren't at all ready to work. They moaned and complained for the first few weeks until I gave them a burst of Brother Kelly's Irish temper. That quieted them down, but I still got a lot of sighs and martyred looks. (Nobody is as good at disgruntled facial expressions as a group of sophomores!)

Despite the bumpy beginning, as the year went on, I could actually see the sophomores growing up and, one day in January, I came to realize that my attitude toward them—and their attitude toward me—had changed completely. We were actually beginning to like each other. There was, unfortunately, one exception, and he seemed simply obstinate. One day when he was complaining, another sophomore turned to him and said, "If you would just shut up and do the work, you'd find that it's not that bad. Why don't you grow up?" I was dumbfounded! I was the one who was supposed to give the lecture, but I had a sophomore alleviating me of that responsibility. From that day on I had a very mature and hard-working class.

There will be many days in his high school career when

your son's time schedule for growing up and your time schedule for his growing up will be at odds. That's the time to remind yourself that you probably had the same conflict with your parents when you were growing up. And you landed on your feet! So will your son. I have never understood how the parent of a teenage boy could be an atheist. How could you get through your son's adolescence without prayer? You will pray daily for his safety and for his well-being, but more often than not, you will probably pray for patience—patience for yourself and patience for him. In your son's good time and in God's good time, your son will grow up. You might pray, as well, that your hair isn't completely gray before that happens. While you are at it, please pray for all of us at Mount Saint Joseph.

Oh, and as for the Salafia boy, he's over forty now and, judging from his entry in the alumni directory, I'd say his mother had nothing to worry about.

On Good Parenting, Good Schooling and God's Grace

When I began my career at Saint John's High School in 1971, I taught next to Brother Jean Meaney, a Falstaffian character who was doing his second tour of duty at Saint John's. He taught at the school in the 1940s and, during his second assignment in his classes, he had the sons of many of the men he had taught during his first assignment. One day, through the classroom wall, I heard him bellow in a voice which matched his girth, "Tremblay, your father was a pain in the butt in 1947, and you're a pain in the butt today." There was then a moment of silence before Brother Jean gave one of his deep belly laughs and commented, "At least we know that you're legitimate!" I remember wondering at the time if I would ever be in the position of teaching sons of former students. Well, I am certainly old enough to do that, but I have never stayed in one place long enough for that to happen. I think that when I leave the Mount, I will go back to a place that I have already been just so I can repeat Brother Jean's line to Tremblay. I always thought it was a great line.

Despite the fact that I have not taught the sons of my former students, I have had some significant contact in the last month with men whom I taught many years ago. I was invited to Saint John's for an awards dinner for a man whom I taught in 1971 and who was being honored as a distinguished alumnus. Of course he's 48 years old now, and I wonder where those 32 years went. I was also invited back to Xavier High School in Connecticut to see another former student receive an award. Actually, I went not so much to see him as to see his mother who taught at Xavier for 15 years. The revered Mrs. Hancock was every principal's dream. She was competent and completely dedicated to the boys in her classes—and she loved her principal! Her son, Greg, has a son who is about to start at Xavier. In both of these instances, I was overwhelmed by how wonderfully my former students had grown up. I can say quite honestly that, when I meet former students, I usually find them to be a credit to the schools from which they graduated and a credit to Xaverian education. Good parenting, good schooling and God's grace can work wonders! In many ways, this has been a rather nostalgic month for me as I've spent time visiting with men whom I haven't seen since they were boys.

As I write this, we have just finished the senior retreat. Seventy-three seniors joined seven members of the faculty at the Clagget Center outside of Frederick for a weekend retreat. That retreat was one of the most wonderful experiences of my brief career at Mount Saint Joseph. As I listened to these young men share their stories and reflect on their experience at Mount Saint Joseph, I was overwhelmed by their goodness. To see them about to graduate from the Mount, so very proud of all that they had accomplished, was a very heartening experience for me. Good parenting, good schooling, and God's grace were certainly evident in the seniors on that retreat. Since I have been in a rather reflective mood recently, I began to think about the potential that these young men have and about the good that they will be able to accomplish in their lives. I doubt that I will be able to meet them again in 30 years as I have done in the past month with some of my former students. I will probably be pushing up daisies in the Brothers' graveyard by then! They, however, will have become faithful husbands and good fathers and a credit to the Mount. I am as sure of that as I am of anything.

The Diary of a Country Priest by Georges Bernanos is one of my favorite novels. I read it every year when I make my retreat. It is about a young priest who is struggling to shepherd a rather difficult country parish and who finds the apathy of his parishioners very discouraging. He dies at the end of the novel and, although he had been at the bedside of many people as they were dying, he dies without a priest present to give him a final Holy Communion. When his friend comments on how sad it is that he will die without Holy Communion, the priest replies, "Does it matter? Grace is everywhere." I firmly believe that. Grace is everywhere because God is everywhere, always at work in every moment of our lives.

It was a long winter, and this school year has had, for me anyway, some very discouraging moments. I think God knew that I needed to have my faith in teenage boys restored. I am usually pretty upbeat about the kids and the potential in each of them, and I know that the bumps and bruises of adolescence are only part of their journey to manhood. I just needed to be reminded of what I have always believed. Seeing some of my former students and watching the seniors on retreat were truly moments of grace. You and I don't really need to worry too much about your son's future. Good parenting, good schooling and God's grace genuinely work wonders, and God's grace is, indeed, everywhere.

On Rogue Male Elephants

It might have been on the Animal Channel or the Discovery Channel, or perhaps it was in *National Geographic.* I can't remember where I discovered that there is a problem in Africa with rogue male elephants. They travel in packs and terrorize not only other elephants, but all wildlife. The problem seems to be that these rogue male elephants grew up in a herd where there were no older bull elephants to teach them proper male elephant behavior. Apparently, in a herd with older bull elephants, when young males act improperly, the older bull elephants literally knock them into line to show them what is proper male elephant behavior and what is not. Even elephants need father figures in their lives!

While a boy knows instinctively that he always has his mother's love, he doesn't always feel that way about his father's love. Boys, and men as well, can feel that there is something about a father's love which has to be earned, and while I don't really think that is true, in the father-son relationship there is a distinction, in my mind at least, between love and respect. A boy may have his father's love simply because he is his father's son, but he does have to earn his father's respect. That is probably not such a bad thing. I have often thought that many of us, as men, spend a good part of our lives trying to live up to our father's expectations. A boy learns to become a man by watching his father. It is one thing that his mother really can't teach him, and it places an awesome responsibility on dad. Childless man that I am, I take my hat off to fathers who struggle every day, year in and year out, to be good role models for their sons. I applaud the fathers who never miss one of their son's games or practices or band concerts or whatever. Being there is what is important.

Once, when I was on retreat, my spiritual director said to me, "You must have had a wonderful father. You have such a positive image of God the Father." That caught me by surprise because my father, although I loved him dearly, was, like all fathers, not perfect. But as I thought about it, I realized that, in many ways, my spiritual director was right. My father was always there. I could talk to him about anything. He was a calm, quiet, steady presence in my life as I grew up. A man of few words, he would come home from work every day, have dinner with my mother, my sister and me, and then he would read for the rest of the night. Both my sister and I are voracious readers. We learned that from watching our father. Largely a self-educated man, he wanted my sister and me to have the education that he didn't have, and I suspect that we both became teachers because our father so valued education. Of course, when I was a teenager, I realized none of this. It wasn't until I was well into my forties, after my father had died, when I began to understand the influence he had on me. Sometimes, when I am talking to kids, I hear my father very quietly in the background.

I can't write about the role of a father in a boy's life without also taking my hat off to the many single mothers we have, not only at Mount Saint Joseph, but at every school at which I have been stationed, who are struggling to raise their sons without a strong male presence in the family. These women have to be both mother and father, but over the years, I have discovered that many of them find a way to bring a male influence into their son's life, whether that be a grandfather or an uncle or a family friend. These mothers know that their sons need strong male role models. I remember a mother at Saint X who told me, when she enrolled her son as a freshman, that she was sending her boy to school there because he needed strong male role models. "His father has let him down so many times. I need him to see that all men don't do that." Of course, I was a bit nervous, hoping that the male faculty at Saint X wouldn't let him down as well. I suspected that they wouldn't, but we are all human, and we all have bad days. As I watched the boy through four years, I realized that we had done for him just what his mother hoped. He had teachers and coaches who didn't let him down. The same thing happens every day at Mount Saint Joseph as I watch our faculty interact with the boys in classrooms, in the cafeteria and on the playing fields.

Back to rogue elephants and a boy's need for his father to teach him how to become a man . . . . Having to earn dad's respect isn't a bad thing for a boy as long as he knows that he always has his dad's love. When Jesus was baptized, the voice of God the Father came from the clouds, saying, "You are my beloved son. In you, I am well pleased." Dads, make sure that your son knows that you and God feel the same way. Happy Father's Day!

On Wise Fools and Parental Endurance

I will never forget Mrs. Buddeke who, in anguish, once asked me, "Where has he gone, that thoughtful and considerate boy who was my son? He's been replaced by a surly know-it-all whom I don't recognize!" Distressed as she was, I hastened to assure her that her thoughtful son would return somewhere in the middle of his junior year. He was simply taking his sophomore hiatus from "thoughtful and considerate boy."

Every year at the "opening of school" class assemblies, I tell the sophomores the sad story of my sophomore year in high school. Although that was forty-one years ago, I still bear the scars! During my sophomore year, I got into a battle of wills with my English teacher, Sister Mary Seretina. Emerging triumphant from that skirmish, Sister Mary Seretina banished me to the principal, Sister Mary Adelbert, and I retreated in defeat with my tail between my legs. My father had the good sense not to get involved, telling me, "You got yourself into it. You get yourself out of it." It was my mouth that had gotten me into trouble and, every year, I tell the sophomores that, if they would only learn to think before they speak or act, they would have a far better sophomore year than I did. Unfortunately, it is a trait of sophomores not to listen to adults. Even as a sophomore in high school, however, I had begun to learn that a smile and my inherent Irish charm could get me out of a number of scrapes. I tried to work my magic on Sister Seretina, but she had seen too many sophomores come and go in her long career to be impressed. She wanted my attitude to improve, and because she wasn't backing down, improve it did.

In Greek, the word sophomore means "wise fool." While some sophomores never go through the "sophomoric" stage, most sophomores have it to some degree. The good news is that they grow out of this stage, usually by the middle of their junior year. This stage, however, can be an endurance test for parents, particularly if you are experiencing sophomoritis for the first time. You live in terror that he will get stuck in this stage. Don't worry. He won't.

All that being said, I really do like sophomores. They are feisty, and I get to use my favorite line on them. I've perfected my delivery over the years, giving them back a bit of the attitude they might have been silly enough to give me. "Your father may have to tolerate that tone of voice from you, young man, but I am not your father, and I don't." Of course, neither does his father. Sister Mary Seretina didn't tolerate it from me forty-one years ago, and we both survived my sophomore year in high school just as you will survive your son's.

The payback, of course, will come twenty-five years from now when you get to watch your grandson put his dad through the same grief his dad gave you. Then you will have the luxury of being doting grandparents who can smile and take your grandson's side. Not long ago, I got a good chuckle from a Mount grandmother who had put four boys through the school. She noted that the son who gave her the most trouble growing up was getting paid back in spades by her beloved grandson, and she was enjoying every minute of it. Keep that in mind on the days when your son is driving you crazy. It will help you to cope!

By the way, Mrs. Buddeke's thoughtful and considerate son did return. I taught him in his junior year, a fine student and a nice young man. He's working in Texas now and doing quite well for himself.

On Electronic Leashes and Parental Surveillance

During the winter of the 1994–1995 school year, I was sitting in the Saint X gymnasium with the late Brother Conrad watching a basketball game. On that winter night, Brother Conrad was visiting Saint X from Florida where he had retired. A Xaverian legend, Brother Conrad had been the Prefect of Studies at Mount Saint Joseph in the late 1950s, the Principal of Saint Joseph's Preparatory School in Bardstown, Kentucky in the early 1960s, and from 1965 until 1974, the Principal of Saint X. When he left Saint X, he returned to Mount Saint Joseph as a teacher.

As we watched the game on that winter night, a Saint X junior passed by and said, "Hi." Brother Conrad looked at the boy and commented, "You must be Marty McDermott's son." The boy was rather nonplussed, and so was I. I wondered how Brother Conrad would know Shawn McDermott. Brother Conrad continued, "You look exactly like your father when he was a 16-year-old boy. I remember him very well from when I was principal here." Not all boys would be delighted to be told that they look like their father, but it was obvious that Shawn was quite pleased. His father, a Saint X grad, was a Louisville policeman at the time. Those were the days before cell phones were annoyingly popular, and I noticed that Shawn had one attached to his belt. I asked him if it was an adolescent status symbol. He replied, "This is no status symbol. It's my father's electronic leash. I have to answer on two rings and tell him where I am." It was then that I became aware of the possibility that cell phones could be used as a means of parental surveillance.

In addition to cell phones, with the preponderance of *Facebook* and other social networking sites, parental surveillance has become ever more important, more challenging and more time-consuming. When I was a young man, the sins of one's youth were forgiven and forgotten. Thanks to the wonders of modern technology, those days are gone forever. Teenage boys do not see ten minutes ahead, so talking to them about ten years from now falls on deaf ears. Nevertheless, I have tried to pound into your sons' heads that what they post now on the Internet could come back to haunt them in ten years. The Internet is eternal, and their lack of judgment as a teenager could be lurking in the shadows of technology. The job of school teachers and parents today is to protect teenagers from themselves. To that end, you need to be sure that your son "friends" you on his *Facebook* page, and you need to monitor what he is posting. The very fact that you are his "friend" may deter him from posting things which might haunt him later. Will he like this? Of course not! But your job is to be his parent and not his best buddy. This task takes on a life of its own when we enter the dog days of summer.

As I write every summer, remember the adverbs: WHERE, WHEN, WHY, HOW and UNDER WHAT CIRCUMSTANCES something is said, done, given or shown. Whenever your son goes out during the summer you should know WHERE he is going, WHEN he will return, WHY he is going there, HOW he is going to keep in touch with you and UNDER WHAT

CIRCUMSTANCES his plans might change. (This is where cell phones can be good electronic leashes!) You also want to know WITH WHOM your son is going to do everything that he is going to do. Let me add here that your son should have a curfew, a reasonable curfew, but a curfew nonetheless. Bad things happen to teenage boys late at night and early in the morning. No good can come of a teenage boy being out all night or into the wee hours of the morning. Also, do not let your son attend large adolescent parties, even if those parties are allegedly chaperoned by adults. There will be drinking and God knows what else, and the adults chaperoning will probably know nothing about it. I know that I sound jaded here, but I have survived thirty-nine years of teaching adolescents. I know what I am talking about.

Many years ago, when I was Principal of Xavier High School in Connecticut, I had a mother tell me at graduation, "When my son started as a freshman, I thought your letters to parents were harsh. After living through the past four years of my son's adolescence, I have realized that you are not at all harsh. You are simply realistic. Believe me, I have been grateful for the ammunition you have given me." After a Mount Saint Joseph Mothers' Club event at which I had spoken, J.T. Farcosky of the Class of 2003 came up to me and said, "Why do you keep giving my mother more ammunition? Every time you talk to the mothers or write those letters, you give her more ammunition to use against me." I smiled and told him that I did it because both his mother and I loved him and wanted to keep him alive and well. Grudgingly, he admitted the truth of that statement, but he said that he didn't have to be happy about it.

I wonder if, 20 years from now, when I am an old Brother

visiting the Mount from the old Brothers' Home, I will recognize J.T.'s son at a Mount Saint Joseph basketball game like Brother Conrad did Shawn McDermott. If I do, I bet that J.T. will be raising his boy just the way his mother raised him and, please God, let there be a headmaster at Mount Saint Joseph 20 years from now who will still be giving J.T. and the other parents the ammunition they need in their daunting, but beautiful, task of raising a son.

ON COLD WINTERS AND WARM MEMORIES

> Winters must be so cold for those who have no warm memories.
>
> DEBORAH KERR TO CARY GRANT IN
> *AN AFFAIR TO REMEMBER*

On the Senior Leadership Retreat in August, as he encourages the seniors to become involved with the Mount during their last year, Mr. Fitz tells them, "On graduation night, when Brother hands you your diploma, you won't be able to make any more memories. Make sure that you make them now and during the year, so that you can cherish them on that night." Making memories! Nothing can warm the heart on a cold winter night like a warm memory. This thought came to me as I was cleaning files recently. I am a pack rat, hoarding letters, papers, lesson plans, God knows what else, thinking that one day they might come in handy. Whenever I receive a grateful letter from a student or a former student, I keep it, so that on those days when I am discouraged, I can rekindle some warm memories. As I was cleaning my files, I discovered a card from a boy whom I taught at Saint X and who is preparing to be a teacher. In the card he wrote, "I hope I become a teacher just like you." I thought to myself, "On my good days, kid! You don't want to be me on my bad days." Nonetheless, rereading the card gave rise to some very warm memories of my years at Saint X.

It is not just the students at the Mount who need to make memories during this year. You need to make memories with your son, becoming a part of his Mount Saint Joseph education. You will regret it twenty years from now if you miss anything involved with him and with his education. The Mother-Son Communion Breakfast, the Father-Son Communion Breakfast, the Junior Ring Mass, the Honor Society Induction, any games or plays or concerts with which he might be involved, the festivities surrounding graduation and any parent programs which we run are all opportunities for you to make memories with your son. Teenage boy that he is, your son will probably grumble and tell you that you do not need to attend everything, but believe me when I tell you that he does want you to attend. He wants to see you in the church as he gets his ring. He wants to hear you in the crowd applauding when he is playing in the band or acting on the stage or participating in a sport (but, please no yelling at the refs!), and he wants to know that you care enough about his education to contact his teachers when things might be going awry.

To make my point, let me tell you a story. At one National Honor Society Induction at Xavier High School in Connecticut many years ago, I was sitting next to Brother William, the moderator of the Society (and a Mount Saint Joseph grad). A young man got up to read and did a beautiful job. I asked Brother William who he was. Giving me the boy's name, he commented, "Wonderful boy! You would kill to have a son like that if you weren't a Brother, but his father isn't here tonight. Never comes to anything that his son does. Too busy! Imagine being too busy to come to your son's induction into the National Honor Society." Now, I am not picking on fathers here because I actually have several mother stories with the same point, but Brother William, on that night, was so on target. Everybody in the room that night was proud of what a fine job the boy had done, but his dad wasn't there to share in the joy and to make a memory.

"Winters must be so cold for those who have no warm memories." You are going to have plenty of cold winters before you are done. Make some memories with your son this year; when you are in the old folks' home, you will be warmed by those memories and the winters won't seem so cold.

On Recognizing Contrition

O, my God, I am heartily sorry for having offended You,
And I detest all my sins because
I dread the loss of Heaven and the pains of Hell,
But most of all because they offend You, my God,
Who are all good and worthy of all my love.

Pre-Vatican II Act of Contrition

Normally when I receive anonymous letters, I consign them to the trash, but a few weeks ago, I received from a mother an anonymous letter which I felt was more than worthy of my consideration. In the letter, the mother noted that I have always recognized the very special bond that exists between a boy and his mother. His mother is the one a boy counts on to love him no matter what. My anonymous mother, however, while recognizing that fact, lamented that her son never says he's sorry when he hurts her because he knows that his failure to apologize is not going to change her love for him. The following week I read the anonymous letter to the student body as part of my Monday morning Pep Talk. I suggested that there are 1,050 boys in the school and that the letter could probably have come from 1,049 of their mothers. Perhaps there is one boy in the school who apologizes to his mother when he hurts her feelings, but even that might be stretching it. I further suggested to the student body that the five most important words in the English language are "I was wrong. I'm sorry."

It's an unfortunate thing that teenage boys don't often realize how much good will they can engender by a simple apology. It's also a sad fact that they can frequently see apologizing as a sign of weakness, for there is certainly something in our culture which reinforces in their minds that apologizing is weak. Given that fact, a parent would do well to look for different signs of contrition than verbal ones. I have enough faith in the boys at the Mount to know that they know when they're wrong. I also know that I have to look for signs of contrition. While they may not be able to articulate their sorrow, they can show their sorrow in other ways. You might dub this the "bull in the china shop" method of apologizing. If you discover that the dishwasher has been emptied when you thought that your son didn't even know you had a dishwasher, that's a teenage boy's "I'm sorry." If he volunteers to look after a sibling whom on most occasions he'd like to send to the moon, that's a teenage boy's "I'm sorry." If he stops to say a few words to you on his way in or out when he hasn't really said anything significant to you in months, that's a teenage boy's "I'm sorry." If he tries to say something to you which doesn't seem to make any sense, it's probably an apology. If he gives you an unexpected hug, that's definitely a teenage boy's "I'm sorry." If you're his dad and he gives you an unexpected hug, you've really hit pay dirt with an unspoken apology. You need to note that these unspoken apologies will not happen immediately after the offense. They may happen a month or two later. Teenage boys are slow processors when it comes to emotion.

When my irascible Irish temperament gets the better of me and I lose my cool with one of the Mount boys, I will usually call him down within a day and apologize for my overreaction. I make it clear that I'm not apologizing for taking him to task, but for the manner in which I did it. I can usually count on an "I'm sorry, too." If someone leads the way, he can follow pretty easily. The best example that you, as parents, can give your son is to apologize on those rare occasions when you overreact. Apologize, but don't beat yourself up over it. You can't deal with teenage boys without overreacting at some point. They are masters at pushing adults into corners.

Once, a boy who had gone seriously astray and who had hurt his parents very deeply said to me, "I've been trying to say I'm sorry to them for the past month, but they just won't listen to me." I suspect that his attempts at apologizing were probably very halting, and I also suspect that his parents' anger at the initial offense was so deep that they were having a hard time interpreting the apology. My advice to the boy on that day was, "Show them you're sorry."

Of course, this is all grist for the mill of Lent, a time that the Church sets aside for prayer and penance. I've always loved the Act of Contrition which we learned in my pre-Vatican II Catholic childhood because it recognizes very clearly that contrition can have a multitude of motivations. We can be sorry because we have hurt someone who is "worthy of all our love." That was called "Perfect Contrition." We can be sorry because we dread the consequences. That was called "Imperfect Contrition." I remember as a boy thinking that it was rather sporting of God that He would settle for imperfect contrition.

When your son hurts you, watch for subtle signs of contrition. It's probably the only subtle thing a teenage boy will ever do. And never forget that, although he doesn't show it very often, he knows that you are most definitely worthy of all his love. Then again, if he's sorry for what he did only because you have grounded him for a month, you still have to forgive him. After all, if imperfect contrition is good enough for God, it has to be good enough for you.

On Opening the Door

> Behold, I stand at the door and knock. If anyone hears my voice and opens the door, then I will enter his house and dine with him, and he with me.
>
> Revelation 3:21

I have a vivid childhood memory of a picture which hung in my grandmother's bedroom, a picture of Christ knocking on a door. Although I don't know the artist's name, I have since learned that it is a fairly well known picture and that there is an interesting story which surrounds it. Apparently the artist's son was somewhat cynical. He must have been a teenage boy! When his father had completed this beautiful picture of Christ, the son rather snidely remarked that his father had forgotten to put a doorknob on the door. The father replied that he had done that quite deliberately because Christ will never force himself on us. When He knocks on the door of our hearts and our lives, we have to open the door from within. In the hectic pace of my life, I wonder how often Christ is knocking and, because I'm so busy, I fail to hear Him. The ironic thing is that I'm supposed to be busy doing His work. The wonderful thing about God, however, is that He is incredibly patient and can wait until He finally gets our attention.

We Catholics are a sacramental church. You may remember the old Baltimore Catechism definition of a sacrament: An outward sign instituted by Christ to give grace. The definition is rather cold, but the reality of the sacraments is anything but cold. Every day when the Church offers the Eucharist, Christ is present, teaching us by His word and nourishing us with His body and blood. Every Sunday, Christ knocks and we have the opportunity to open the doors of our hearts. Unfortunately, it's an opportunity that many Catholics don't take, and I'd like to suggest, hopefully in a gentle manner, that it is one of the opportunities which you, as parents, owe to your son. I must admit that I find it somewhat discouraging when I discover the number of Mount students who don't attend Mass regularly. Sometimes they tell me, "Well, my parents don't go. Why should I?"

I think I've probably heard every reason that there is for not attending Mass. I once had a father tell me, when I was in the act of expelling his son, that he would never attend Mass again because I was a completely uncharitable and unchristian man. At that point I laughed, further irritating him. I just couldn't imagine that anyone would allow his relationship with God to depend on me. Most religious attend Mass very frequently during the week, but there was a point in my life when, because I was chagrined at the priest, I avoided attending Mass during the week and only made my Sunday obligation. My spiritual director at the time, Sister Florence, was a very wise woman. When I explained all this to her, she said, "I've never heard of a Mass where Christ failed to be present to the worshipping community because of some defect on the part of the priest." I couldn't imagine the father of the boy whom I expelled letting me determine his relationship with God, yet I had once allowed a priest I didn't like control my relationship with God. It certainly doesn't make much sense.

Getting a teenage boy to attend Mass (or Sunday services if you are not Catholic) willingly can be a monumental task and one you might shrink from tackling, but you will have a far better chance if you are being a good example by faithfully attending Mass yourself. As his parents, you have the right to insist that, as long as he lives in your house, he obeys your rules; attending church regularly should be one of those rules. He may sit there and pout through the entire service, but he will know that it's a value his parents cherish, and that will ultimately have its effect. I can't tell you how many times I've seen former students of mine come back to the practice of their faith when they marry and have their own children. They realize then, quite clearly, that they can't raise their children without God. They may have fought their parents when they were teenagers, but as adults, they come to appreciate the value of the faith in which they were raised.

So, the next time you are tempted to play golf on Sunday rather than attend Mass or to sleep late because you've worked hard over the week, ask yourself if you are being a good example to your son by golfing or by sleeping. I suspect you know the answer. Christ stands at the door and knocks. By your own example, teach your son how important it is to open that door.

On Blessings and Curses

There are times when I think that I am like Pavlov's dog. All it takes is one sophomore to give me a little adolescent backtalk or, worse than that, the "You poor pitiful adult, how dare you correct me" look, and the Kelly temper erupts in all of its Irish glory. If my temper has been somewhat of a curse, the blessing is that I have a remarkable ability to forgive and forget. All that it takes is a simple apology from the miscreant, and all is forgiven and forgotten. I have had seniors say to me, "Do you remember when I was a freshman, and you took me on for a fare-thee-well?" I never remember. I probably didn't even remember the day after the incident. Usually I discover, once I calm down, that the boy who is the object of my temper is really a very nice kid who just made a tactical error.

One of the things I have learned over the years is that an occasional burst of adult pique can have a dramatic and salubrious effect on a teenager, but if the fits of pique come too frequently (and too loudly!), the teenager shuts down and pays no attention. That is something I have had to learn over the years, and my bursts of temper are pretty infrequent now, just frequent enough to remind the student body that I have a temper. Years ago in Connecticut, in my early days as an Assistant Principal and as a Principal, my temper got the better of me far too often. I realized that one day when I walked into the cafeteria and the kids became quiet. They had become wary of my temper, and that did neither them nor me any good. While I have always joked that the day that I can't silence the cafeteria with a good bellow, I will know that it is time to retire, I have learned to be more patient with the hubbub that comes with boys at the feeding trough.

Another thing that I have learned over the years is that you have to be very careful with your words when you are talking to teenagers because, once a word has been said, it cannot be taken back. Teenagers can say hurtful things to us adults, but we adults can also say hurtful things to teenagers when they have backed us into a corner or pushed us over the edge. I always tell young teachers that they have to remember that, in any negative interaction with a boy, they are the adult and he is the boy. In some respects, he has a right to act like a boy, but the adult always has to act like an adult. I can also think of a few notable failures during my career in that regard. I have branded into my memory the look of pain on the face of a young man over twenty years ago whom I called a loser. If I could have taken those words back at the time, of course I would have, and I am pretty sure that I apologized immediately. But once a word is spoken, it is spoken.

You owe this month's letter to three Mount sophomores who set off my Pavlovian reaction by "the look." Actually, it was just one boy, and his two friends got caught in the crossfire. As always, I told them to see me the next day when I had calmed down. They did, and, as always, they were good kids who had made a tactical error. I suspect they have learned that when the Brother President asks them a question, they had best answer in a civil tone.

It is the nature of teenagers to drive us adults crazy. That is their job in life. We adults, however, need always to be careful with our tempers and with our words. But even as we attempt to do that, we don't always succeed. It is then that we need to remember the words of Saint Francis de Sales, "Be patient with all things, but first of all with yourself." And, of course, learn to forgive and forget. That's a lesson boys can teach us. They're pretty good at it.

On Aunts and the Resurrection

Shortly before he died at the age of eighty-five, my father, who was an incredibly smart man, said, "The smartest thing that I ever did was to marry into your mother's family." I knew exactly what he meant. My mother came from an extremely close knit French-Canadian family where anyone's problem was everyone's problem. My grandparents emigrated from Quebec in the late nineteenth century to Worcester, Massachusetts, where they had nine children, six of whom lived to be adults. They brought their children up, as many immigrants did in those days, retaining their French-Canadian customs and the French language. My grandparents obviously did something right in raising their children because the bond among all of their children was profound. As I grew up, if anyone stubbed a toe in my mother's family, aunts would appear out of nowhere bringing food and comfort. Although my mother was the youngest, she died first at the very young age of sixty-six and, at her death, two of her sisters, my Aunt Juliette and my Aunt Yvonne, immediately began to take care of my father. They would arrive at his house monthly to cook and clean and to let Dad know that he was still very much a part of the Vigneault family. They were with my dad on the night that my mother died.

While my mother only lived to be sixty-six, all of her siblings lived to be at least ninety. Last January, the last two of my mother's sisters, Aunt Juliette and Aunt Yvonne, died within three days of one another. Aunt Julie was one hundred one years old and, Aunt Yvonne, ninety-seven. Julie was as sharp as a tack until the day she died and, shortly before Christmas, I visited her in the nursing home. She had decided that it was time to go home to God since all of her friends were dead and her sister, Yvonne, was lost in the clouds of Alzheimer's disease. As she planned to go home to God, however, she did have one request she wanted Him to honor. She said, "I want God to take me and your Aunt Yvonne at the same time. I don't want to be in heaven worrying about her." I told her that I thought one doesn't have to worry in heaven, but she gave me a look that said quite clearly that, if she were in heaven and Aunt Yvonne was still on earth, she would worry.

Aunt Julie had never married, while Aunt Yvonne had married, but never had children. Her husband, Uncle Frank, died very young. When he was dying, Aunt Julie took him and Aunt Yvonne into her home to help care for Uncle Frank. When he died, Aunt Yvonne stayed on. Of her ninety-seven years, Aunt Yvonne had lived eighty-four of them with her sister, Julie. The day we buried Julie, we got a call from the nursing home that Aunt Yvonne had spiked a fever and appeared to be dying. Because of her Alzheimer's disease, we didn't tell her of Aunt Julie's death since she wouldn't understand, but my cousin, Phyllis, thought that Yvonne, even with her clouded mind, knew that her sister wasn't coming to see her. The day after we buried Julie, Yvonne died. Now, some people would consider this coincidence, but I don't at all. I think it is a sign of my Aunt Julie's clout with God. She got to heaven and told Him exactly what she wanted, and God obliged.

Although I am in the "God business," my faith is only a pale shadow of the faith of my mother's sisters. Shortly before she died, also at the age of ninety-seven, I had a conversation with my mother's oldest sister, my Aunt Alice. She was in a nursing home as well, and she wanted to tell me about her dreams. "I have been dreaming a great deal recently about my parents and about Dot (my mother). They're in heaven, and they're so happy, and they're waiting for me. It is time for me to go to heaven to see Jesus and them." She was almost in a reverie as she spoke and, when she came out of it, she looked at me and remembered whom she was talking to. "Your mother is very happy in heaven," she stated, not as speculation, but as fact. Aunt Alice's dreams had gotten her in touch with eternity where she was longing to be. She did, however, have one complaint for God, which she fully intended to voice as soon as she got to heaven. Her son, my cousin Dick, had developed early onset Alzheimer's and, because Aunt Alice had lived so long, she had to watch it. "No mother should have to live to see her own son not know who she is." She fully intended to make that point with God when she got to heaven. Since then, her son has joined her. Both Aunt Alice and Dick played the piano quite well, so I know there's music in heaven!

I have often thought that, with the very elderly, the boundary between time and eternity becomes somewhat blurred. I have no doubt that my Aunt Juliette and my Aunt Alice were very much in touch with God and with the home in heaven to which they were journeying. As I celebrate Easter this year, I am perhaps more in touch with the resurrection than I have ever been. St. Paul reminds us, "If Christ is not risen, then vain is our preaching and vain is your faith." My aunts knew in Whom they had spent their lives believing, and now they know that their faith was certainly not in vain.

Happy Easter.

On Butterflies and Letting Go

I am writing this letter particularly for the parents of the graduating class. Parents of underclassmen can put it away until their sons graduate.

Last fall, my secretary, Mrs. Drenner, gave me a monarch butterfly still in its cocoon and attached to a clear plastic cup. I watched the seemingly lifeless cocoon for three weeks, wondering if it would ever burst into a butterfly. Lifeless as it seemed, I almost despaired that my butterfly would ever shed its cocoon, yet one morning I arrived at school to discover a beautiful monarch butterfly trapped in the cup. Mrs. Drenner and I took it out into the courtyard between Ryken Hall and Founders Hall, but the butterfly showed no sign of wanting to fly. Finally, Mrs. Drenner put it on her finger and held it up into the air, and then, discovering its wings, the butterfly began to soar into the air, flying in looping circles higher and higher until it reached the top of the Tower and headed over the trees towards the Brothers' House in joyous swoops and twirls. We lost sight of it as it flew over the Brothers' House. I think that both Mrs. Drenner and I were awed at this spectacle, the joyous flight of a butterfly that had found its wings.

Your son may not be a butterfly, but during his time at Mount Saint Joseph, we (his teachers) and you (his parents) have hoped that he would find his wings and that he would learn to fly on his own. As this year's seniors graduate, I am sure that the parents of the graduates have some very mixed feelings. While you take joy and delight in all that your son has accomplished, you are also aware that he has found his wings and that he is ready to fly on his own. It is never easy to let go to allow him to do that. You have nurtured him and protected and taught him for eighteen years and, now, in a very real sense, some of the bonds which tie him to you are going to be broken. While you can be very proud of the man he is becoming, letting go of the boy he was can be difficult.

For the parents of the graduating class, these last four years have gone by very quickly. Before you know it, he will have graduated from college, started his own life, and established his own family. All of these are things for which you have raised him. If your son has found his wings, it is because you gave them to him; your greatest gift, once he has graduated from the Mount, is to let him use those wings.

I was very touched recently when the mother of a former student of mine told me that she had saved all of my letters during her son's four years at school and that she planned to give them to him the day that he becomes a father. While her words touched my heart, they are also a beautiful recognition that she knows why she gave her son his wings. Of course, you may not want to think about becoming a grandparent just yet!

Letting go isn't easy, but remember the butterfly in its joyous flight. May your son find his wings and may you and Mount Saint Joseph be very proud of his flight.

On Having a Heart in the Right Place

There was once, in Connecticut, an old and holy priest who was worshiped by his parishioners. He was not a great celebrant of the liturgy. In fact, he could get rather confused as he said Mass and frequently left things out. Neither was he a great preacher. While his sermons were incredibly sincere, they were somewhat convoluted. He was devoted not only to his parishioners but to Xavier High School and to the Xaverian Brothers at Xavier. On one occasion, when he had a heart attack, he came to live with us for a month and edified the entire community by his faithfulness to prayer and by his kindness. He always volunteered to be a confessor at school retreats. The Sacrament of Penance was one place where he absolutely shined. Going to confession to Father Frank was like going to confession to Christ. Despite his limitations as a celebrant and as a preacher, his parishioners did love him because of his holiness. They recognized that, in their pastor, they had the real thing. His heart was in the right place, always with God and with them.

Over the years, I have noticed the same dynamic at work with kids and teachers. The teacher might not be the greatest tactician in the classroom, but if the kids perceive that the teacher's heart is with them, they can forgive his or her pedagogical inadequacies. I am reminded of one of our

Brothers who, for many years in his life, had a very serious problem with alcohol. The boys in his classes and on his teams frequently covered for him because, despite his weaknesses, they knew how very much he loved them. When he found his salvation in Alcoholics Anonymous, he became among the most grateful of men. His heart was always in the right place, and his students knew that.

You are not perfect parents, nor am I the perfect headmaster, but your son and my students are able to forgive us our inadequacies if they perceive that our hearts are in the right place. One of the most troubling conversations I ever had was with Miss Norris, the guidance director at St. X. A boy whom we both knew had just passed us in the hallway, and I asked her if she knew why the boy always looked so sad. She replied, "Because he is about twelfth on his mother's list of priorities, and he knows it." His mother's career was apparently more important to her than was her son. It is very rare that I encounter parents whose children are not their chief priority, but it has occasionally occurred. I wonder if that mother knew that her son knew that her heart wasn't in the right place.

I'm lucky. My responsibility for your son ends, in a very real sense, with his graduation from the Mount. Your job as parents, however, will continue until that day when both you and your children are with God in heaven. You're in it for the long haul! Until then, it is all about having your heart in the right place. If our hearts are in the right place, God can work wonders despite our mistakes. At the last judgment, I don't think that God will judge us on our failures as parents or as teachers. I think He will look to see if our hearts were in the right place.

On Young Love

Recently, I was speaking with a Saint Joe mother about the trials and tribulations of raising a teenage boy. In the course of the conversation, she said, "I thought I was ready for everything, but I wasn't ready for love." What she wasn't ready for was the intensity of adolescent love, the all-consuming obsession that it can become for a teenage boy who is having his first (or second or even third) experience of a serious relationship with a girl. I suspect that, for a parent, such intensity can be disconcerting and even frightening. You, his family, and—on rare occasions—his car, take second place to the new love of his life. If you are lucky, you like the girl. If you are not, you don't. Like her or dislike her, she is a reality with whom you have to deal. I know one couple who are man and wife today (happily married after many years, thank God) because of the intensity of parental opposition to their relationship. At the time, both Sister Mary Agnes, the principal of Mercy High School in Connecticut, and I contended with the parents that, if they did not react so strongly, the relationship would probably go the way of most adolescent relationships and end in a tearful scene at a school dance. Your best bet is to get to know your son's girlfriend, to be welcoming to her and to become acquainted with her parents as well. On the other hand, don't be too enthusiastic about her if you like her. Your son just might need the wiggle room to get out of the relationship, and if you are already talking as if she is a future daughter-in-law, he could feel trapped.

Even as I read what I have just written, I realize that it is all rather confusing. That is because adolescent love is confusing. Of course, Dad (or, failing him, Mom) has to have "The Sex Talk" with him and have it as early as possible. If you haven't done it yet, do it now! You don't want to be closing the barn door after the horse is gone. Will he listen? Who knows! You, however, will have done your part to keep him on the straight and narrow. Early in my career, I had to teach a course entitled "Love, Sex and Marriage." What a twenty-four-year-old celibate who had been in a monastery for six years was doing teaching that course, I will never know. When I taught the chapter on abstaining from pre-marital sex, I made them memorize the reasons in the book, and from the back of the room, I heard one kid whisper to another, "Will somebody tell the poor man that he's too late?" You don't want to be too late.

I am one of the few men in this world who actually learned about sex from his father. My father explained it to me in the same rather graphic detail that he used to explain the internal combustion engine before he gave me my first driving lesson. While he covered all of the aspects of sex, he didn't make it sound terribly interesting. As I think back on it forty-five years later, that was probably deliberate on his part.

One final story. Years ago, a young man who, if I recall correctly, had won the religion award at graduation, had to get married the summer after graduation. As a group of the Brothers drove to the wedding, we were all struck by how such things can happen even to the best of them. If ever there was a pro-life celebration, that wedding was it. And the marriage has lasted!

Talking to your sons about sex, drugs, alcohol and dangerous driving will never be easy, but avoiding those talks is just too bloody risky. When you do have those talks, he will probably dismiss you with a roll of the eyes and a sarcastic, "Yea, right." Don't let that deter you. In his heart, he will know exactly what you are doing and, in his heart, although you will never see it, he will be grateful.

ON HUMILITY

As teachers and as parents, we spend a good deal of time giving direction and instruction to our students and our children. We pray that what we have taught them might make a permanent impression, changing their world view or their behavior or both. As important as it is to give good direction to the young people in our lives, it is equally important to have the humility to learn from them and to recognize that, sometimes, their world view might be more perceptive than our own or their practice might be better than ours. I had a striking example of this during the past summer.

As an English teacher, I am very rigorous in correcting student essays. I smother their compositions in red ink and follow the corrections up with an audio tape on which I give them very clear instructions as to what they have to do to improve their essays. A few years ago, the father of one of my students stopped me at PTA to say that, one night, he heard a man yelling at his son in his son's bedroom. He ran to his son's bedroom only to discover his son listening to a tape on which I had gone off the deep end about his son's deplorable punctuation. (I have been using the "smother and yell" technique of teaching composition for a long time, and the tiger is certainly not going to change his stripes.) Over the years, I have received some very positive feedback from former students about how my methods actually helped them to write better and removed the fear which students can face when confronted with a daunting writing assignment. One former student e-mailed me not long ago to tell me that, when all of the other college freshmen in his dorm were panicking about writing papers, he laughed and told them that nothing that he had been assigned yet in college could match what I had made him do in high school. I must admit I was rather proud about that.

Last summer, I hired a former student to help with the typing of the jubilee booklet which the Xaverian Brothers published for our 150th anniversary in the United States. Not only had living Xaverian Brothers submitted essays for the booklet, but we also dedicated a section of the booklet to historical writings by Brothers long dead. At one point, Sebastian, the student, asked me if he should correct the grammar and punctuation as he typed. I thought that was a little brassy! He was suggesting that he correct the work of men who had taught school for years, all of whom were quite good writers. Nevertheless, I told him that he could take a crack at it. You can imagine my chagrin the day that he handed me an essay which I had written (and which he didn't know I had written), covered in red with various suggestions for better phrasing and punctuation. As I read his corrections of my work, I realized that 90% of them were more than accurate. Now my excuse, which I would never accept from a student, is that I had a lot to write during the summer and that I "batted out" the essays as quickly as I could. Nevertheless, I was humbled by the fact that a former student was able to correct my errors. I was also very proud of what a fine job he had done. His other English teachers and I must have trained him very well!

As I reflect on my thirty-three years as a teacher, I am very much aware that I have certainly learned as much from my students as I have taught them. I suspect that, when you reflect on your son's life, he has probably taught you a great deal as well. Perhaps you are not as jaded and as cynical as I can be on occasions, but there are many times when the goodness and the enthusiasm of the young men at the Mount remind me that "jaded and cynical" is not a very good way to approach life. It all goes back to humility. As our Blessed Mother prayed in her *Magnificat*, "God has scattered the proud of heart and exalted the humble." In Saint Jerome's Latin Vulgate, he translates our Blessed Mother's words "*exsultavit humiles*," which means "God will cause the humble to rejoice exceedingly." We teachers and parents need to be sufficiently humble to learn from the young people in our lives. We still have to teach them and correct them. That's our job! But if we learn from them as well, we might just stay as young in spirit as they are. And God will cause us to rejoice exceedingly because of our humility!

On Family Dinners

I try to keep up with adolescent trends, but, middle-aged celibate that I am, I occasionally miss things about modern family life. A few years ago, I was surprised to discover that family dinners were no longer the norm in the modern family. The active, hectic schedules of parents and children preclude sitting down together for family dinner. Once I became aware of this, many other things that I had noticed about family life began to make sense. Family dinner is the perfect time for communication between parents and teenagers. While the conversation might, at times, be forced by mom or dad, it is still conversation and can provide parents with very good insight into what is going on in their children's lives.

In the January 9, 2005, edition of the *Baltimore Sun,* there appeared an article by Stephen G. Henderson entitled "Happy Meals." In that article, Mr. Henderson quotes a survey which states that, ". . . there is a strong correlation between frequent family dinners and reduced risk that a teen will smoke, drink, or use illicit drugs. What's more, the National Center on Addiction and Substance Abuse reports that children who eat regularly with their families are less likely to have sex at young ages, get into physical fights, be suspended from school or have thoughts of suicide. These behavior patterns hold true regardless of the child's gender or the family's socioeconomic level."

As a youth, family dinner in my house was a sacred time. Once my father came home from work, we sat down to a dinner which my mother had cooked and which my father served. You ate everything he put on your plate. Since I liked everything but lima beans, eating everything on my plate was not the problem for me that it was for my sister, who was a rather finicky eater. (Ironically, she became a professional chef and a college professor of Culinary Arts.) We sat at the table until my father excused us, after which he and my mother had coffee and a cigarette. (In the 1950s you didn't worry about first- or second-hand smoke!) I don't remember dinner conversations, but I am sure that our parents made both my sister and me tell them about our day and what was happening in school. Since my sister was a far better student than I, I probably mumbled a lot when we talked about school performance. After my sister left for college and I found a job, things did change somewhat, but I still remember regular family dinners. Those are very warm memories.

Every day I see boys leaving Mount Saint Joseph very late after practices and games, and I know that many who are not here for extra-curricular activities have part-time jobs which keep them occupied after school hours. Planning family dinners must certainly be a logistical nightmare, but logistical nightmares notwithstanding, the more often you can gather your family for dinner, the better chance you have of discovering what is going on in your children's lives. Teenage boys are not the best communicators, but they do love food, so the creative parent plying their son with food can probably persuade him to talk more than he normally would. When you consider the nature of the teenage male, food as a springboard for communication makes perfect sense.

Be mindful, however, that modern technology can get in the way of family dynamics even when the family is together for dinner. This past summer, my friend Brother Raymond and I were in a restaurant, and next to us sat a family with a teenage son and a teenage daughter. Mother, father, son, and daughter ordered their meals, and then they all took out their BlackBerries and began to text. Not a word was spoken among these four people. Each one was lost in his or her own world, texting God only knows whom. I wanted to go over to their table and tell them to put the silly BlackBerries away and talk to each other. The gentler, non-judgmental side of my nature triumphed on that occasion. I left the family to their texting. What a lost opportunity it was for the parents! Two parents with two captive children, and they were paying absolutely no attention. What we have gained in communication through technology, we've certainly lost in face-to-face discussion and in the ability to communicate in a deeply personal manner. On those occasions when Mr. Fitz and I take students out to dinner, I bark very loudly if I see one of them take out his cell phone. I tell him that it is incredibly impolite to use a cell phone when someone has invited you out and is paying for dinner. They look at me as if I'm a dinosaur.

A few years ago, I attended the funeral of the mother of one of my students; she had died at the very young age of fifty after a long battle with cancer. Since her children were too distraught to speak at her funeral, they had a friend give a eulogy which they had written. Her children recalled how important the family dinner was to their mother and how she would let none of them escape from the table until each had told her about his or her day. As they responded to whatever questions came into their mother's mind while she listened to them, she was discovering exactly what was going on in their lives. Her children had a profound sense of gratitude for that, even as they admitted to complaining and moaning about it at the time.

Make sure that, as your son grows older, you find ways to gather your family for dinner often. Put your Blackberries away and talk to each other. Your son may complain and moan, but, in time, he will be grateful that family dinners were important to you. In the process, you might even develop a few warm memories of your own.

On Saint Joseph and God in the Messy Details of Life

Recently, at a meeting of the Plant Committee of the Board of Directors, we discussed the issue of pigeon manure in the rafters of the Tower. For over 100 years, pigeons found a home in our Tower before we finally installed mesh to drive them away. As I sat there listening to the discussion about pigeon manure, my easily-distracted mind went back forty years to the novitiate. When I was a novice in the Xaverian Brothers, my novice master, Brother Kevin, always spoke about the religious life as a great spiritual journey, a falling in love with the service of God, lived out in service to others. We made our vows "for the glory of the Father and the salvation of men." There was absolutely no mention of pigeon manure.

For a good part of my life, I kept God in a "spiritual box," and I had a difficult time finding Him present in the grittier details of life, like discussions of pigeon manure in the Tower. As I have grown older, that has changed. There is a program on television called *Joan of Arcadia* in which a teenage girl is visited weekly by God, who comes to her in the guise of various men and women. God always gives Joan a task which she doesn't understand at first, but which ultimately leads her to a greater and deeper understanding of life. In a recent episode, God appears as a very well-dressed, middle-aged woman and asks Joan to buy her a latte. As Joan does, circumstances lead her to save a girl whom she doesn't particularly like from certain death from an oncoming car. As the plot progresses, things become very messy for Joan who finds herself at first hailed as a hero and then spurned by the very person she saved. At the end, she complains to God that there is too much complexity, too many contradictions in life. God replies, "But that's where I am, in the complexity and the contradictions."

On March 19, we celebrate the great Feast of Saint Joseph, patron of our school. If anyone knew about finding God in the complexities and contradictions of life, it was certainly Saint Joseph. Told by God to marry his fiancée who was pregnant, but not by him, Saint Joseph had to raise a son who wasn't his in a marriage which God had mysteriously overshadowed. It is my experience that God isn't a great explainer, so I expect that Saint Joseph was caught in a mystery for which God didn't provide much explanation. Lack of explanations notwithstanding, Saint Joseph raised Jesus and was a faithful husband to Mary. When Jesus was lost in the temple and Mary said to him, "Your father and I have been seeking you in sorrow for three days," Jesus replied, "Did you not know that I had to be about my Father's business?" If Saint Joseph was a normal man and father, and I suspect that he was, that remark certainly must have hurt. Once again, God is in the complexity and the contradictions! By the time he died, Saint Joseph must have been a master at fathoming complexity and contradictions.

I always like to end where I began, so as I sat at the Plant Committee meeting, I thought that I could have a good conversation with Saint Joseph about pigeon manure. He would understand. In fact, I suspect that he would point out to me that it is often in those messy details of life, where God is most present if only we know how to look for Him. Somehow God is present in those places where at first He seems most absent, such as in the death of a young father or in a lost job or even in a difficult divorce. Our lives, like Saint Joseph's, are often shrouded in mystery, but it is in the mystery that God is always present.

May Saint Joseph pray for this school which so proudly bears his name.

On Testing the Limits

A recent study confirmed what teachers and parents have known for generations: the adolescent mind is not completely developed when it comes to sound judgment. The study maintains that this lack of development in the brain is one of the reasons adolescents are such great risk takers. Of course, you and I know that testing the limits is a strong suit with the teenage male. Over the years, the Mount has developed appropriate responses to this adolescent strong suit. If a boy crosses the line in a relatively minor way, such as being late for school, wearing his hair too long, acting overly frisky in class or in the cafeteria, or being a tad mouthy, we have JUG, which stands for Justice Under God. In JUG, students stand for an hour in silence facing a wall. There is nothing that a teenage boy hates more than being still and being bored. JUG helps to reinforce in his mind that he has, indeed, crossed the line. If he receives too many JUGS, he is assigned to Saturday JUG. If the two previous tactics don't work, or if the crossing of the line is of a more serious nature, we have suspension and probation. Finally, and we really dislike having to use this option, there is expulsion. Expulsion occurs when a young man has so seriously crossed the line that he can no longer remain at Mount Saint Joseph. It can happen that one offense is so serious we go immediately to this option. Again, we don't like to do that, but sometimes teenage boys don't give us much choice.

One of the great joys of being the President of the school is that I don't have to do the daily discipline. Mr. Fitzpatrick and Mr. Armstrong take care of that. I do remember, however, my days as a principal when discipline was my daily lot. I recall one boy whom I had to expel after I had given him multiple chances. As he left the property, he encountered a group of his classmates who asked him why he was being expelled. He replied, "I backed Brother into a corner and really didn't give him any choice. He had to throw me out." When his classmates told me his response, I thought that maybe, in what seemed to be an irrevocable defeat, there just might have been a tiny victory, for the boy finally took responsibility for his actions.

As parents, you don't have the luxury of all of the options which a school has to deal with testing of the limits. You do, however, have some analogous powers. One old Brother used to tell parents that the best way to punish a boy is to find something that he really likes and take it away for a while. You can take away his car keys, ground him for a weekend or two, or find other ways to curtail his freedom. There is nothing a boy dislikes more than having his freedom curtailed. Obviously, expulsion isn't an option for parents, although at the last Senior Retreat, a boy prayed for a friend of his whose parents were going to throw him out of the house the day he turned eighteen. I can only imagine what a wrenching experience that must be both for the parents and for the son. I have seen it happen in my long career, but only rarely.

One thing that I have learned over the years is that, when you are dealing with an adolescent who has crossed the line, you always have to attempt to remain calm. Now, your sons can tell you that I don't always do that, but God knows I try. You are much more effective when disciplining a teenager if you remain calmly dispassionate. When they find their freedom curtailed, adolescents can say some pretty nasty things. They might tell you that you don't love them and that you are about the worst parent that has ever come down the line. Of course, they don't mean it, but they have to find something with which to strike back. Your best bet is always to remain calmly objective: "You did that; therefore, the consequences are these." You will always do well to set the ground rules with your son before anything happens so that he knows pretty much what to expect if he decides to use his adolescent prerogative of testing the limits.

One of the joys of my late middle age is watching my godson and his wife raise their young daughters. Colin and Tracy shower their daughters with love even as they teach them proper behavior. I know that, when they are teenagers, their daughters will probably test the limits with Colin and Tracy, but even as they test, their daughters will know deep in their hearts how very much their parents love them.

Your son is going to cross the line at least occasionally—or perhaps frequently, depending on his temperament—and, since you are his parents, you are going to bring him back into line when he does. He may not come back into line quietly, but as long as he knows, deep in his heart, how very much you love him, he will understand what you are doing, even though he can never admit it to you. You need to remember that and to keep calm. One day, you will watch your beloved grandson give his dad the same grief that his dad gave you. Parenting does have its paybacks!

On Taking the Keys

At the Father's Club Bull Roast last year, I was discussing teenagers and driving with two of our fathers who had some serious concerns about their sons' driving habits. Once your son has his license and the use of a car, all you can do is hope that common sense will prevail. Of course, you also have to pray! Boys take to cars like ducks to water, but sometimes their common sense can fail them once they are behind the wheel. As the two fathers and I were talking about this, I remembered my most terrifying experience in a car, and it wasn't with a teenager. It was fifteen years ago with my eighty-four-year-old father. We were headed for my cousin's home for dinner in my father's 1978 Thunderbird. My father hadn't driven for a few years because of failing health, but the car in the garage was still a symbol of independence to him. His housekeeper did the driving, and he was usually happy to let her do that. On this occasion, however, he told me that he wanted to drive one last time. I tried to convince him that it might not be a very good idea, but my father was a very stubborn Irishman, so drive he did. For twenty minutes I was in absolute terror as we whipped along above the speed limit, so close to the shoulder that I thought we were going to clip a few trees along the way. He was having a grand time. I kept yelling, "Dad, slow down!" I finally stopped yelling because every time I did, he took his eyes off the road to look at me. When we arrived at my cousin's house, my Irish was definitely up, and I said more than firmly, "Dad, give me the keys!" He did. I suppose that ride could have been payback for the terrors I might have given him when he was teaching me how to drive when I was sixteen. What goes around comes around!

As bad as my father's driving was that day, it could not compare to some of the incredibly dangerous driving I have seen, even on school property, with teenage boys behind the wheel. Convinced as they are of their own immortality, teenage boys can take incredible risks when they are driving, endangering not only their lives, but the lives of everyone else on the road. When you point this out to them, they tell you that they are in perfect control of the car. Having lived through far too many teenage deaths from car accidents in my career, I have no patience at all with this adolescent braggadocio. As your sons can tell you, I am constantly harassing the boys here to make sure that they have fastened their seat belts when they enter a car and to drive carefully and responsibly. As many adolescent deaths as I have experienced, I have also encountered far more boys emerging from a "totaled" car relatively unscathed because they were wearing seatbelts.

Of course, we adults have to be good role models to teenagers as far as driving is concerned. Over the years, on at least two occasions during my Monday morning pep talks, I have confessed to the student body that I have been guilty of negligent driving. In one instance, I had received a $100 speeding ticket on I-91 in Connecticut (and I was pretty sure that some of the students in the school at which I was stationed had seen me pulled over by the police!), and last year, I regretfully informed the student body at the Mount that I had killed Bambi's mother on Frederick Road because I was talking on a cell phone as I drove, rather than paying attention. Deer do have a way of darting out onto a road. I still feel quite badly about Bambi's mother.

However strict or lenient you are with your son in other matters of discipline, take this one bit of advice from the cranky old celibate who runs your son's school. If you ever hear that he has been driving recklessly, take the car keys away for a good long time. Pay no attention to his screaming and hollering and his claims that you don't love him. It is far better to have him angry with you than to have him dead. I realize that sounds harsh, but as I have already said, I couldn't begin to count the number of teenage wakes I have attended because of car wrecks. Consider this a somber reflection for your day.

Every time he leaves the house, tell your son to use his seatbelt and to drive carefully and responsibly. If you hear that he has neglected either of these things, do what I did with my Dad. Take his keys away!

On Having No Regrets

At least three times in my long career as a school administrator, I have had to tell a boy that one of his parents had died. As you can imagine, that is a dreadful experience. I have indelibly etched in my memory an occasion twenty years ago at Xavier High School when I had to perform this sorry task. I honestly can't remember the boy's name, so let's call him Joe. Joe's father had been seriously ill, and as soon as Joe came into my office, he looked at me and said, "He's dead, isn't he?" I replied that he was and asked Joe to sit down. After a moment of silence, he said, "I never told him how much I loved him. You see, we used to fight a lot." Realizing that what I said next was crucial to Joe's well being, I offered a quick prayer to the Holy Spirit, asking God to give me the right words. Trusting that the Holy Spirit wouldn't let me down, I told Joe that his father knew that he loved him and that he didn't have to worry about that. Of course, Joe wanted to know how I could know that. I replied, "Don't forget that your father was a son, too. He probably fought with his father even though he loved him, so I'm pretty sure that he knew that you loved him even when you were fighting." I then asked Joe if he was Catholic, and when he replied, "Yes," I told him that it was time to put his faith into practice. As a Catholic, Joe believed that his father was now with God, and because his father was now with God, his father knows all of those things that were unspoken. Whether or not that consoled Joe, I don't really know. I do know that I tried. Losing a parent when you are a teenager is a very difficult thing. Actually, losing a parent at any age is a very difficult thing.

Once a year, during my Monday morning pep talk, I tell the story of Joe, and I remind the kids how important it is for them to tell their parents that they love them. I know we have some boys at the Mount who probably tell their parents that they love them every day, and we have others who probably haven't said it in a very long time. They all need to be reminded. Last year one Mount student lost his mother, and another, his father. On both of those occasions I reminded the kids about the fragility of life and again encouraged them not to pass up the opportunity of telling their parents that they love them. Whether or not my admonitions succeeded, you would know better than I. Of course, you have to give them a good example. Every day you should tell your son that you love him. I think with mothers it's almost instinctual, but it is very important for fathers to speak those words as well. Boys can get it into their heads that there are some things that men don't do, but if a boy hears his father telling his mother that he loves her, and if he hears his father saying the same to him, he will learn that a man can and should express affection for the people he loves.

November is the month of All Saints, when we pray for those whom we loved who are now with God. How much better to tell the important people in our lives that we love them now, while we have them with us. The "Saints" in our lives know of our love, because they are with God and now know everything, but I bet that, even in heaven, they would like to have heard it on earth!

Every day, tell your son that you love him. If your parents are still alive, tell them, too! If you do that, then, unlike Joe, you will have no regrets when those you love go home to God.

On Good Advice and the Young

During the very peaceful and spiritual four months of my Sabbatical, I had occasion to think about how frequently good advice is wasted on the young. You and I give your sons a great deal of good advice. You probably give him a daily dose, but since your son doesn't have your adult experience, he doesn't understand how good the advice is. Both you and I would like him to learn from our good advice so that he might save himself from some of life's pitfalls. Unfortunately, teenage boys are determined to learn from experience rather than from what adults tell them. You and I spend a great deal of time praying that their experiences will be helpful and not harmful to them.

The fact that good advice seems to be lost on the young was brought home to me quite clearly during my Sabbatical when I realized that some good advice that was given to me thirty-four years ago was wasted on my youth. As an undergraduate, I majored in Latin and Greek and, while I learned my Latin when I was fourteen years old, I did not begin Greek until my sophomore year of college. By the time I graduated, I felt that I was a far better Greek student than I was a Latin student since I could read the New Testament in the original Greek as if it were English. During the second semester of my senior year at Catholic University, I had the magnificent Doctor George Siefert for a course in Homer. I'd already had Doctor Siefert for at least three courses in Latin, and I was delighted that I was going to end my college career having this incredibly demanding, but absolutely brilliant teacher once again. Shortly before graduation, he gave me some very good advice. He said, "Brother, Greek is such a complicated language that it is very easy to lose. You have worked hard to learn it, so you don't want to lose it. If you do your spiritual reading in the New Testament every day in Greek, you will never lose your Greek. This is very good advice I'm giving you which I hope you take." Now, I had enough sense to realize that it was good advice, but once I graduated from college, I began teaching and my life became very busy. I was teaching three different subjects in the course of each school day, coaching (very poorly) cross-country and track, and moderating a number of other school activities. By the time the day ended, doing my spiritual reading in Greek was the last thing on my mind. Doctor Siefert's good advice was lost on me.

Fast-forward thirty-four years, and I am on Sabbatical studying scripture with some marvelous teachers. They make references to the original Greek of the New Testament, and I discover that it is Greek to me. I look at pages of the New Testament in Greek and can barely read a word. If only I had listened to Doctor Siefert! Deciding that I was going to try to pound Greek back into my head, I became very frustrated and only somewhat successful. Unfortunately, learning something at fifty-eight is far more difficult than learning something at twenty-one. The difficulty I had re-learning my Greek was one of those "mortality moments" when I realized that I am growing older and slower, both physically and intellectually. Doctor Siefert is probably smiling in heaven at my foolishness in not taking his good advice so long ago.

So, should we adults stop giving advice to the young? Definitely not! There is always the remote possibility that they will actually listen to us and save themselves a lot of grief and heartache. Failing that, they will at least recognize, once they have the experience, that the advice we gave them so long ago was, in fact, quite good. It will help to validate their experience, once they have it. Perhaps, twenty-five years from now, when your son is raising your grandson or granddaughter, he will think to himself, "Mom and Dad were right about that. Why didn't I listen to them?" Of course, your son may never tell you when he finally recognizes that your advice was good advice. He doesn't want to give you the opportunity to say, "I told you so!" So keep giving that good advice even if your son doesn't appear to be listening. I certainly intend to keep giving good advice to the Mount Saint Joseph student body even if they appear to sleep through my Monday morning pep talks. Some of your good advice and my good advice will certainly penetrate that adolescent façade and will perhaps one day bear some good fruit that you and I won't see. But God will see, and that is all that matters.

On Understanding Our Parents

Listening to a feature story on National Public Radio one afternoon, I found myself in a reflective mood. NPR was doing a program on families separated by the war in Iraq. During the program, a young soldier was interviewed who, through satellite telephone, was able to listen to his wife giving birth to his twin daughters. Both he and his wife spoke of the heartache of being separated at such a moment, since these were their first children after a long struggle with infertility. The wife spoke of the fear she had that her husband would never hold his daughters and that his daughters might never know their father. Fortunately, the husband was granted a compassionate leave during which, at least for a brief time, he was able to help his wife care for his daughters before he had to return to Iraq.

As I listened to the story, I had a startling revelation about my parents, realizing for the first time in my heart something I had known intellectually for years. They say that the longest journey is from the head to the heart. I can stand as a testimony to that!

My father was deployed to Europe during the Second World War when my mother was three months pregnant with my sister. My sister was three years old before my father ever saw her, since he remained mobilized for a year after the Armistice which ended World War II. As I listened to the NPR story, I began to understand for the first time what my parents had to suffer. My mother was left to endure most of her pregnancy and the birth of her first child without the support of her husband. Fortunately for her, my mother came from a very large and very close-knit family. She had the support of her parents and her siblings, but parents and siblings certainly couldn't make up for her husband and the father of her child. I suspect my mother wondered if my father was ever going to see and hold his daughter. Those must have been three long and lonely years as my sister took her first steps and spoke her first words without her father to witness it.

And what must it have been like for my father who had only pictures of his daughter? I am sure that he probably wondered if he would ever see or hold her. Tim Breen, of the Mount Saint Joseph faculty, is a bit of a military historian, and he has discovered that my father belonged to an elite counter-intelligence unit, the members of which had to take a vow of silence for fifty years about what they did during the war. I often wondered why my father never spoke of the war, until Mr. Breen informed me that my father couldn't. My father apparently took a promise to be silent and, to my father, a promise was sacred. He kept it until the day he died, because he died before the fifty year period was up. When he wrote to my mother during the war, he couldn't tell her where he was or what he was doing, which certainly must have added to her anxiety (and probably his). I am only now beginning to realize what they must have gone through.

Is there a lesson in this? I think that parents often want their children to understand them and to understand something of what their struggles have been in life. That is perhaps asking too much of teenagers, and maybe it is even asking too much of adults. One day, it may just dawn on your son, as it has dawned on me, what the deeper meaning of your life has been. My mother has been dead for twenty-five years, and my father, for twelve. It is only now in recent years that I have regretted all of the questions I never asked them. But that is just the parent-child relationship, I guess.

To end on a less serious note, my mother often told me that, as a precocious six-year-old, I discovered there were far more pictures of my sister as a baby than there were of me. I wanted to know why! Apparently my mother explained to me, on any number of occasions, that Daddy was away at the war when Patty was born, so he needed pictures to see what she looked like. Daddy didn't need pictures of me because he was there for my birth and my first words and my first steps. Apparently I wasn't convinced by my mother's logic. War or no war, I thought that there should have been at least as many pictures of me as there were of my sister. Sibling rivalry starts young, but I suspect that you have noticed that.

The ultimate question, I suppose, is how well any of us have appreciated the gift our parents have been for us. Taking time to talk to one's parents is well worth the effort. If you do that, you won't have some of the regrets I had after both of my parents died. So much left unsaid!

On Growing Up

Recently, I visited a 1986 graduate of Xavier High School who lives in San Antonio with his wife and three sons. Chris is a pediatric surgeon in the Air Force. I had last seen him in 1991 when he was a newly married medical student at Johns Hopkins here in Baltimore, and I was stationed at our Provincialate in Ellicott City. Twenty years is a long time ago, but I do remember that, as a junior and a senior in high school, Chris had a number of lapses of judgment which required that his father come in for a conference with me. Chris remembered the details far more clearly than I did, but on one occasion, he and some friends had decided to have a large adolescent party for which they had hired a senior on the football team to serve as the bouncer. Somehow, Sister Mary, the principal of Mercy High School, caught wind of this since Mercy and Xavier were only a mile apart and the two schools formed one community. It was a co-ed group which planned this party, and Sister Mary and I summoned the perpetrators to her office. Sister Mary was a perfect lady when dealing with the girls, but I must admit that I wasn't a perfect gentleman when dealing with the boys. I seem to recall ripping into Chris with a vengeance, probably because it was his second offense. The first offense I can't actually remember, although Chris remembers it quite clearly. Anyway, parents were summoned, and the kibosh was put on that adolescent party. God knows that there were probably ten other parties in the same season of which we knew nothing. As a side note, let me remind you that, if you allow such parties in your home, you do need your head examined. I'll never forget the parents who were arrested after one such party and charged with allowing minors to drink in their home. They probably didn't know minors were drinking in their home, but they were.

Anyway, back to my point. Every day, you deal with your son's lack of common sense and his, at times, rather immature approach to life. You probably become frustrated on occasion and wonder if he will ever grow up. Well, I am here to tell you that he will grow up. Look at Chris. I suspect that, in high school, I always knew that he was a very good boy, even though he lacked common sense. Some of the things that he did probably could have warranted what Winston Churchill called "The royal order of the boot," but I never expelled him because I must have thought that he just needed to grow up. And now he is a pediatric surgeon! Grow up he did, right on schedule, just as your son will. On those dark days when you are wondering if you are going to have a forty-year-old adolescent on your hands twenty years from now, take heart thinking about Chris. He is only one story. I have a thousand of them, stories of kids who showed very little sign of growing up in high school but who ultimately became mature and productive adults. There must be four or five chapters in my book, *Respecting the Man the Boy Will Become,* giving examples of this adolescent to adult phenomenon. If you want more examples, the book is for sale in the bookstore!

Living as they do in San Antonio, Chris and his wife don't see their families as often as they would like. Their two-year-old son was incredibly affectionate, and he kept asking me to pick him up, which I did. At one point I heard him ask his mother, "Is that man Grandpa?" Apparently he doesn't see his Grandpa as often as he would like! His mother replied that I was not Grandpa. I was Daddy's old principal (. . . emphasis on the "old," since I am more than old enough to be his grandfather). As I left their house, memories of twenty years ago made me chuckle. When I was yelling at Chris in Sister Mary's office so many years ago, it would never have crossed my mind that, twenty years later, his son would be wondering if I was his grandfather. Life has a way of playing its little jokes on us.

Take heart! Your son will grow up and, unlike me, you actually will have the opportunity to become Grandma and Grandpa. Judging from my friends who are now grandparents, I would say that being a grandparent is a piece of cake next to being the parent of a teenage boy who is trying to grow up. Just remember that he will grow up.

On Unfathomable Mysteries

I once told you the story of St. Augustine who, walking along a beach while trying to fathom the mystery of the Holy Trinity, encountered a young boy digging a hole in the sand. When Augustine asked him what he was doing, the boy replied, "I'm trying to put the ocean into this hole." Augustine told him that he was undertaking an impossible task. To this the boy replied, "I'll put the ocean in this hole before you understand the Holy Trinity." I've always maintained that the boy had to be a teenager.

Lately, I've been thinking about unfathomable mysteries, and foremost on my mind is the mystery of boys and toilets. Why is it that boys can't flush toilets after they've done their business? If I had a nickel for every toilet that I've flushed in every men's room in every school in which I have been stationed over the last thirty-five years, I could lower our tuition. Of course, women might add to that mystery by asking why it is that men can't put toilet seats down after they're done. Again, it's just unfathomable. As I continued to reflect on mysteries and boys, I wondered why they can never keep their shirts tucked in and why general sloppiness is the order of their day. I once had dinner at the home of a family whose son I taught, and he showed me his room. In his closet he had all of his clothes perfectly aligned by color and use. I turned to his mother and said, "You know that he's not a normal boy." To this she replied, "I know he's not. His brother is the normal boy. Let me show you the chaos of his room." I would be willing to bet that most of you have normal boys and general chaos.

This past summer, a rising senior at the Mount arrived to talk to Mr. Fitzpatrick and, as both Mr. Fitz and I looked at him, we noticed that something was quite odd. He only had one eyebrow. When Mr. Fitz questioned him about this, he told us that he'd shaved off his right eyebrow because he wanted to see what it would look like. Of course, it looked silly. There is another mystery for you. Why do they do silly things for which there is no reasonable explanation except in their minds? Again, I would be a millionaire if I had a nickel for every time I've said to a boy, "What in the name of God were you thinking?" Of course, bright as they are, they weren't thinking! Envisioning consequences is not a boy's strong suit.

More mystery. Why do you have to drag information out of them? Why, when asked a simple, direct question, do boys grunt in reply, or why, when asked what they did or learned in school on a given day, do they reply, "Nothing"? Nothing?! You perhaps wonder why you are paying his tuition if he is learning nothing. I've actually heard this reply from boys whom I taught during the day. When I ask if they remember our discussion of appearance and reality in Shakespeare or tension and resolution in the poetry of John Donne, they modify their answer to, "Oh, yeah! We learned that."

I was once asked if I would consider working in a co-educational school. My reply was immediately negative, not because I have anything against girls, but since it has taken me thirty-five years to figure out boys, mysteries notwithstanding, I don't think I have enough years left to live in which to figure out girls. I will stick with boys and what I know!

Even as I mention the mysteries about boys, I can honestly say that, every year in August, I look forward to the coming school year with a great deal of joy and excitement. Working with boys, despite their mysteries, is an incredibly rewarding task. Very often (but not always!) what you see is what you get—no mystery there! Once you understand that, the rest is a piece of cake.

On Jerome and Perspective

Recently, I had dinner with a young man, Jerome, whom I taught during my first year at the Mount. Now a senior at the University of Maryland, he has matured in a way which made his old teacher quite proud. As we were talking, he reminded me of an incident during his senior year which I had totally forgotten. Jerome played hockey for the Mount for four years and, in the last game of his senior year, he was benched by Coach Terwilliger. Reflecting on that incident, he said, "At the time, I was furious with the coach, but now I have the greatest respect for him. For whatever reason, I hadn't been playing well, and that was hurting the team. Coach Terwilliger knew that the team was more important than my ego and didn't play me. That was a valuable lesson for me to learn about teamwork." I wanted to take out a tape recorder and have him speak into the microphone, so that I could play it back for future parents and students at those times when high school athletic careers are not going as parents and students might like. It's really all about perspective, isn't it?

When I first became a principal in 1982, the redoubtable Sister Rose Burns, a Sister of Saint Joseph and battle-scarred veteran of high school administration in Catholic schools in Massachusetts, told me that, as I began my principalship, the three banes of my existence would be music, maintenance and athletics. After twenty-three years as a headmaster, to her list I would add technology, but she certainly hit the target on the first three. Sister Rose had eliminated hockey in a Massachusetts school because of declining enrollment and financial problems. In Massachusetts, eliminating hockey is as close to heresy as you can get, and I suspect that poor Sister Rose, holy nun that she was, was probably burned in effigy at a number of hockey rallies.

Over the years, I've had countless conversations with kids and parents about keeping perspective, not just on athletics, but on life in general as it is lived out by teenage boys in high school. High school is a place to learn valuable lessons—academically, spiritually, athletically and socially—and some of those lessons can be tough for a teenage boy to learn. Being cut from a team or not being given the playing time that he thinks he deserves can be hard on him and on his parents who obviously want him to succeed. Not achieving the grades he might want or not being accepted at the college he might choose or learning to cope with a very rigorous teacher can be difficult as well, but they can also prepare him for the "slings and arrows of outrageous fortune" which life is going to offer him.

In her novel, *The Jane Austen Book Club*, Karen Fowler writes, "Sylvia thought how all parents wanted an impossible life for their children—happy beginning, happy middle, happy ending. No plot of any kind. What uninteresting people would result if parents got their way." You want your son to be happy, with no disappointments and no failures—just success and blue skies. Of course, you realize that's impossible. It's not even Christian! Our Lord made it very clear during his life that the Cross is part and parcel of the Christian life. I can guarantee you that your son will learn far more from his failures than he will learn from his successes. Our failures can teach us valuable life lessons, but like my former student, Jerome, we need the perspective of time to learn those lessons. When your son meets the "slings and arrows of outrageous fortune," your job as parents is to help him gain perspective and to see what might not be obvious to him at the time. He won't learn the lesson when you are trying to teach it, but he will remember, and, like Jerome, he may well learn it five years later. It's all about perspective.

Oh, and one parting comment. Your son will never learn perspective if you don't have it. Teenage boys listen to our actions far more than to our words, which makes it tough for us adults. We have to "walk the walk," not just "talk the talk" if we want them to pay attention. Perspective: If you have it, your son will learn it. And that's just the way it is!

On Holding on to Faith

> May He support us all the day long, till the shades lengthen and the evening comes, and the busy world is hushed, and the fever of life is over and our work is done! Then in His Mercy may He give us a safe lodging and a holy rest and peace at the last.
>
> Cardinal Newman

Displayed in my office since 1991 is one of the few pieces of original art I own, a beautiful sculpture, entitled "The Sorrowful Parents," which depicts Mary and Joseph grieving over the dead body of Christ. Yes, I know that Saint Joseph was dead when Jesus died, but he certainly had to be there with his wife in spirit at the most sorrowful moment of her life. I had the sculpture crafted because, during my nine years as Principal of Xavier High School in Connecticut, nine boys who were present students in the school died, and I spent a great deal of time with sorrowful parents. The sculpture, in many ways, has become a symbol for me of the far too many times I have attempted to console grieving parents on the death of their son. I learned very early on that there is absolutely nothing I or anyone can say to a parent who is experiencing every parent's worst nightmare. The support of your presence is all you can offer. Only a parent who has been through such a horrible event can possibly understand what newly-grieving parents are going through.

When I first went to Saint Xavier High School in Louisville in 1993, we did not have a student die until my third year as President. That first boy was one whom I had taught and whom I knew very well. Once again, I was speechless in the presence of grieving parents. The school swung into action and planned the boy's funeral. Speaking at the Mass, I told the parents that I realized there was nothing that I or anyone else could say to them. I could only hope that the presence of the Saint X community provided some consolation to them.

This is very much on my mind because of the recent death of Colin Curley, a graduate of the Mount Saint Joseph Class of 2002 and our freshman lacrosse coach. Through his wake and funeral, Mount Saint Joseph did what it could to support the Curley family with the presence of the school community. I hope that presence was consoling.

Early on in my career, a wise old nun gave me this advice about dealing with grieving parents: "Tell them to pray to the Blessed Virgin. She knows what it is to have lost a son, and she can console them." I have often thought that is wise advice. Through the wonder of grace, Mary can console while we are at a loss for words.

Every Sunday at Mass we proclaim that we believe in "the resurrection of the dead and the life of the world to come." We believe that firmly, but it can be difficult to remember when we are overwhelmed with the pain of loss. It has been said that faith is only really faith when it is all you are holding on to. I can only imagine how hard it is for grieving parents to cling to faith. When my beloved cousin, Honey, was dying of cancer at the age of fifty, one of the last things she said to me was, "I'm hanging on to heaven by my fingernails." In the dark times of life we are, like my cousin, often holding on to our faith by our fingernails. But even as we hold on, our God is there with us.

May the Mother of God be with all of those parents grieving the loss of a child and may Christ our Savior give all who have died "a safe lodging and a holy rest and peace at the last." AMEN.

On Finding the Right Balance

While so many stories begin "Once upon a time," I realized not long ago that many of my letters to you begin, "Long ago in another school far away." Well, this is one of those letters.

Long ago, in another school far away, there was a young man in my senior English class who had a serious attendance problem. Unfortunately for him, I was also the principal of the school and had more clout than the average teacher. The boy's mother was a single parent, struggling to bring up a number of children, and she was beside herself with her oldest son who seemed to be having some serious emotional problems. Getting him out of bed and to school was a major undertaking. One morning she called me in despair, and I drove to the boy's home. With his mother in tow, I burst into his bedroom yelling, "Get your butt out of bed. Get dressed. You are coming with me to school." The boy, of course, was rather startled, but I was relentless. I went with his mother back into the living room while he dressed, and when he didn't come out as quickly as I would have liked, I went back in to discover him sitting on the side of the bed smoking a cigarette. The tirade began again; eventually he got dressed and I drove him to school. When we got out of the car, I said to him, "Don't make me do that again." Now, I had just finished a master's degree in counseling, and you would think that I would have had better counseling skills than I exhibited on that long-ago morning. I was stuck between his depression and my desire that he graduate from high school on time. Determined that he would graduate with his class, I hounded him into coming to school. I have learned a lot since then and certainly would act differently today. Those were simpler days.

One of the tensions that we face as a school and that you face as parents is knowing exactly when to be tough and when to be lenient. "Tough love" has become one of the catch phrases of our age. Over the years, I have learned by instinct that there are some boys who are, by their nature, "rough and tumble" and who respond best to rather strict discipline, while there are others who are more fragile and who need gentler handling. I usually go on my gut, but my gut has been wrong. Teenage boys are masters of disguise, and you don't always know what is going on inside of them. Some of the most seemingly together boys can actually be not together at all, and some of the scruffy and seemingly less than together boys can be solid as rocks. You know your children well, and you have to make a judgment about how to discipline them and keep them in line. I know nothing about girls, but I can tell you that boys do need to be kept in line, one way or the other. A boy who wanders from the mark can get himself into far too much trouble today, so vigilance on the part of his parents is essential.

Not long ago in this school, I sent a boy from my classroom to the office to get a book. As soon as he had left the classroom, I heard a hubbub in the hallway and discovered that he, seeing two other boys pushing a large television cart down the hall, had decided to jump on the cart for a free ride. I bellowed, and he went scampering. In that instance, I made an immediate judgment that he was one of the "rough and tumble" boys who just needed a good, swift kick in the butt. With others, I might have been a bit gentler.

You need to be very vigilant with your son, and you need to keep him in line. He has to get to school on time, behave himself, do his work, and obey you and your house rules. How you see that he does all of those depends on his personality and your relationship with him. There are some parents who think that they need to treat all of their children exactly alike. I think that is just silly because sons and daughters are not exactly alike. We probably have 80 sets of brothers at the Mount, and no two or three brothers are ever alike. One of your sons may need the good, swift kick in the butt, while another needs the arm around the shoulder and the consoling word. To make it more confusing, the same son may need a kick in the morning and a consoling word in the afternoon.

Whatever path you take, I would remind you that your son needs a parent and not a friend. If you can manage parent and friend, you are truly blessed. If you can't, choose parent. Friend can come later. My mother, God rest her soul, and my sister fought like cats and dogs when my sister was a teenager, yet, before my mother died when my sister was thirty-six, they had become the best of friends. The same will hold true with your son if you just give it time.

And to conclude, the boy long-ago in the school far away did graduate.

On a Spring Afternoon at the Mount

On the rare occasions when I do the afternoon announcements, I end by saying, "Ready, set, go home!" The odd thing is that they do not go home. There are days when one would get the impression that the Mount is still a boarding school, as it was from 1876 until 1960, because the boys stay here long after dismissal. There are some who actually do seem to live here!

Come and take a walk with me about the campus on a beautiful spring day. In room 206 of Saint Joseph Hall, Dr. Pease is teaching Italian to a group of eight boys. There is no course credit involved here. These are just young men who want to learn another language. At the other end of the spectrum, in room 208, we have the boys in JUG who are copying the Mount book as just punishment for their sins. When I ask why they are there, I am given the standard list of school boy sins: late for class, late for school, cheating, no absentee note or a scuffle in the hallways. Mr. Bonham is the JUG master on this day, and one boy whom Mr. Bonham is tutoring in Religion is indignant that I have mistaken him for one of the Jugged. In the Guidance Center, Miss Coyne, our Director of Student Activities, presides over a group of seniors who are working on their senior project and two groups of boys who are playing games of chess. For reasons I don't quite understand, the Guidance Center is where the boys gather to play chess. In the Library, every one of the twenty-five computers is in use while Mrs. Byron watches over her afternoon flock there. (Mrs. Byron goes back to the days when the legendary Brother Donald was the Mount's librarian.) In the cafeteria, Mr. Harris prefects all the boys who are waiting for rides, some of whom are here with her until six in the evening. There are card games going on, music being played and the general hubbub of sixty boys letting off steam. I always tell the business manager that whatever we pay Mr. Harris, it isn't enough!

As I walk over to the gym, I meet one senior who is late for track practice. He explains to me that he is going to attempt to run track and sing in the school musical at the same time. I tell him that keeping both Mr. Constantine and Mr. Hartsfield happy is an impossible task, but what do I know? I've only seen it a thousand times before! As I walk past the tennis courts, I ask Mr. Hughes if he has made all of his cuts. He has. Seeing a boy I have in class on the team, I ask Mr. Hughes if he is any good. To this Mr. Hughes replies, "We'll see!" The boy just smiles. On the track, Coach Constantine is taking attendance. The senior I had already encountered arrives just in time to yell, "Present!" when his name is called, and he starts ripping off his clothes as he runs to the locker room. The "weight men" on the track team, those who will throw the discus and the shot, are obvious by their size, and the lankiness of the long distance runners is obvious as well. Brother Charles appears to be late for practice. He is usually at his place near the pole vault pit by now, wearing his straw hat and singing to the boys as he coaches. He must be down in the bowels of the gymnasium, collecting or passing out uniforms.

Leaving the gym, I head for the baseball field where Mr. Shearer and Mr. Schultheis are taking their final look at the freshmen. Unfortunately, hearts will be broken today when the final cuts are made. That's part of a boy's life in high school, and I say a quick prayer that those who are cut will find something else to do among the plethora of activities we offer at the Mount. I am a firm believer that if God closes a door, He opens a window. I hope those who are cut will find the open window.

On the lower practice fields and on Slentz Field, it appears that half of the school is out for lacrosse. That makes sense since this is Baltimore! Outside the Development Office, a group of boys waiting for rides play touch football. Mr. Fitz always calls that area "the playpen," since many of the kids gather there after school simply to toss balls around and play various pick-up games.

It is a real joy for me to see the youthful enthusiasm of all these Mount students on a spring day. I always tell the kids not to be an 8:00 to 2:30 student, to find a niche at the Mount and to make it a second home. As I walk the campus, I see not only our present students, but I also feel the presence of boys playing on these grounds and of the Brothers coaching and prefecting them fifty, one hundred, and one-hundred-thirty years ago. The tradition lives on with this generation of Mount men and with our wonderful faculty. Brother Dominic, the first principal, must be smiling in heaven. I know I'm smiling on earth!

On the Adolescent Journey

I had not seen Christopher Bradley since he graduated from Xavier High School in 1989, nor did I know that he was living in Maryland and working as a State Trooper. His parents, Dennis and Rosemary, were very much involved with the Home School Association at Xavier High School when I was the principal there, and I have very fond memories of all the Bradleys. They have remained particularly close to Brother Lawrence Harvey, the Director of our Xaverian Brothers Sponsored Schools here at the Brothers' Generalate on the campus of the Mount. Dennis and Rosemary were visiting their son and his family from their retirement home in Florida and, when they stopped by the Mount to see Brother Lawrence, he invited me to have lunch with them. Since I had not seen Chris in 18 years, my memories of him were of a fine teenage boy. I was incredibly impressed with the man he has grown into, a devoted husband and father. Dennis and Rosemary's loving pride in their son and in their grandchildren was a beautiful thing to behold, even during a rather brief lunch.

It is not often that I get to see how my former students have grown up, but when I do, I feel some of the pride that you, as parents, must feel as you watch your son grow and mature. Every year at graduation, I am amazed at how the fourteen-year-old boys whom we admitted to the Mount four years ago have matured into young men of whom the school can be proud. Mr. Fitz and I meet with all of the seniors during the spring semester, in groups of twenty-five, to ask them about their experience at the Mount. I am overwhelmed during these meetings how very well they understand the lessons the Mount had to teach them. For some of them, they will readily admit that those lessons came later in their career at the Mount than earlier, but learn them they did. You can see it in the way they treat each other and in the way they treat the underclassmen. At one of the meetings, I spoke about a disciplinary incident that had concerned me, and one of the seniors replied, "That had to be an underclassman, Brother. We know better than that." He was right on both counts.

Many things have changed since I began teaching in 1971. There are some things about boys, however, that never change. They enter as wide-eyed freshmen, a little frightened, but enthusiastic about the bigger world of high school. It takes them about a year to settle in, but once they do, the very fact that they feel at home leads them to become moderately cynical, know-it-all sophomores who make all teachers work for their money. I remember when I first started teaching, I had some wonderful groups of freshmen whom I liked very much and who liked me. I couldn't understand, when they became sophomores, why they wouldn't speak to me in the halls or didn't seem at all happy to see me. My mentor, Brother Ivan, told me that was just sophomore boys, and that they would be happy to see me again when they were juniors. He was right! At the beginning of junior year, we see reason and personality returning, and by the end of the junior year, they usually show remarkable signs of maturity. That is one of the reasons why I have always loved teaching juniors. You can watch the growth during the year. As seniors, they begin to understand what we have been trying to teach them during their first three years, not just academically but spiritually. I see some very fine young men in the senior class whom I took to task when they were sophomores. That "sophomore boy" is long gone and a very mature, right-thinking young man is now the reality. It really is fun to watch. Of course, I don't have to live with them!

While I was visiting with the Bradleys, Chris told me that he is also a member of the Maryland National Guard and about to be deployed to Iraq for a tour of duty that will last over four-hundred days. I can't begin to imagine how his parents, his wife and his children must feel at this moment. I ask you to pray for Chris and to pray for all two-hundred seventy-nine young men who will graduate from the Mount this month. They are well on their way to becoming men of whom this school and their parents can be gratefully proud. Their growth process may have given their parents and us some gray hairs, but the end product is well worth the effort.

On the Spectrum of Faith

Last month, I was asked to give a retreat for the alumni of Saint Michael's High School in Brooklyn. The Xaverian Brothers ran Saint Michael's from 1926 until 1960 when it closed, so the youngest alumnus of Saint Michael's is sixty-five years old. At the retreat, there were men from the Classes of 1933 through 1960, a wonderful group of men who impressed me incredibly with their faith and their devotion to the Church.

The night before I gave the retreat, I met with two former students, Jason and Chip, in New York for dinner. I had taught both of these men years ago in Kentucky, and since I am always delighted to see former students, I very much looked forward to having dinner with them. As we shared memories of the time we spent together at Saint Xavier High School, the evening was as delightful as I expected it would be. At one point, however, the conversation veered off to religion, always a dangerous topic. Jason is a practicing member of the Eastern Orthodox Church. Brought up by an Irish Catholic mother and an Eastern Orthodox father, and having attended twelve years of Catholic schools, he opted for Eastern Orthodoxy over Roman Catholicism. His twin brother, Eli, married a Catholic woman and did just the opposite. Chip spoke of his desire to be a faithful and practicing Catholic, but he told me he had great difficulty with some of the pronouncements of the American hierarchy and their attempts to influence politics. Since I have given forty-two years of my life to the Church and, since I love the Church dearly with all its imperfections, I tried to point out to him the difference between faith and religion, that faith in Jesus Christ can transcend the very human elements of the Church. Jesus' disciples, saints that they are, certainly had their human faults and failings as they attempted to lead the early Church. Saints Peter and Paul even disagreed publicly! But Christ is the bedrock, and on Him we rest in faith.

The conversation with these two young men intrigued me because they were both obviously men of faith taking a different path in their search for God. But they are searching! The next day, I met with the alumni of Saint Michael's who ranged in age from sixty-five to ninety-two. For these men, there was no dichotomy between faith and religion. As I spoke to them, their faith in Christ and their love for the Church were palpable to me. They loved the Church, warts and all, and their faith in Christ is as bedrock as it can be. They also love the Xaverian Brothers, the men who taught them and who provided them with the very firm foundations on which they have based their lives. I found it a humbling experience to speak with men of such faith and such devotion.

You might say that, in twenty-four hours, I experienced two ends of a spectrum, a spectrum that contained youth and old age, the search for faith and faith found, journeys beginning and journeys coming to an end. Infused throughout this spectrum, and permeating it completely, is God, who understands the struggles of the young and the peace of the elderly.

I can only hope that we instill in the young men at the Mount the seeds of faith which will germinate slowly throughout their lives and ultimately flower as they have in the men of Saint Michael's. The inculcating and developing of faith are far more important than their GPAs or the colleges which accept them. As an elderly nun once said to me, “It’s nice that you made the Dean’s list, but did you make the Lord’s list? That’s the only list that really matters.” The Xaverian Brothers founded the Mount in 1876 to transmit the faith to the coming generation. We haven’t changed our mission one iota in one hundred thirty-one years, and I pray that we never will. Struggle with his faith your son will. That’s normal! Let’s pray that, when his struggles are done, he will find himself indelibly inscribed on the Lord’s list, the only list that really matters.

On the Subjunctive of Attraction

In Latin there are three "moods" for verbs: the indicative, which is the mood of fact, the imperative, which is the mood of command, and the subjunctive, which is the mood of possibility. Latin has an intricate set of grammatical rules as to when to use the subjunctive. My favorite is the "subjunctive of attraction." I explain to students that the subjunctive of attraction is about a weak-willed indicative verb. Indicative verbs are far stronger than subjunctive verbs since they state fact and not possibility, but occasionally you have a weak-willed indicative verb which finds itself surrounded in a sentence or paragraph by subjunctives. It feels out of place and wants to follow the crowd, so it becomes subjunctive for no good reason other than it doesn't want to stand out in the sentence. This poor indicative verb doesn't have the strength of its convictions. Rather than assessing itself as the strongest verb in the sentence, it follows the crowd, a much weaker crowd at that, and becomes a subjunctive.

Of course, you see where I am leading with all of this. One of the problems of dealing with the adolescent male is that he does not like to stand out in a crowd as being any different from his peers. This is not a bad thing if he is running with a good crowd, but it can become tragic if he's running with a bad crowd. Every year in one of my Monday morning pep talks,

I tell the students at the Mount about two former students of mine who are in jail for murder. One was a boy whom I would never have picked as a potential murderer when he was a student in school. He was a very nice young man, quite involved in the school, but unfortunately he associated with the wrong crowd and suffered tragic consequences.

One of the first stories I shared in *Respecting the Man the Boy Will Become* told of a time, years ago, when I was a young teacher at Saint John's High School and one of our students committed a serious crime. He was in the county jail and the Superior of the Brothers' Community, Brother Ivan, was dispatching two young Brothers to visit the boy. As they left, Brother Ivan said, "You'll be in the first pew proud as a peacock when one of your old boys says his first Mass. Well, in the pulpit or the prison, they are all ours, and we do not abandon them in their need." I thought that was a wonderful lesson for young Brothers to learn. In my own career I have ridden in the back of police cars with boys being arrested, visited jails and written countless letters of support for young men in trouble. We know of a Mount graduate in prison whom Brother Declan, prior to his death, visited monthly for years. You might say that fidelity to those who have gone astray is also part of the Xaverian Charism.

While we remain faithful to those who have strayed, our main job in a Xaverian school is to keep the boys on the right track, to teach them that each one has to be his own man and that he does not have to follow the crowd. He needs to be able to judge the moral character of his friends and determine if they are people with whom he should associate. The faculty and staff at the Mount try to pound these things into your sons' heads. While I think we are more successful than not, boys will be boys. They need constant reminders about judging the quality of their acquaintances and about not following the crowd. When you remind your son of these things, he may dismiss you as a cranky adult, but don't stop! Somewhere, deep in his conscious mind, he knows when he is following the wrong crowd, and he knows the possible consequences. Keep reminding your son to choose his companions wisely, to choose friends who have the right values and who will lead him in the best direction. Remind him that he can be a leader, taking others in a proper direction as well.

Grammarian that I am, both in English and Latin, I want a school full of strong indicative verbs. No weak subjunctives for Mount Saint Joseph! And certainly no subjunctives by attraction. Together, let's work to make sure that your son becomes a strong indicative verb, a leader who isn't afraid to stand up for what he believes.

On Listening Children

What do you leave to your child when you are dead?
Only whatever you put in its head
Careful what you say
Children will listen

Stephen Sondheim from *Into the Woods*

We think that our sons and our students don't listen. In fact, not listening seems to be an adolescent strong suit. Fortunately or unfortunately, that's not really accurate. Adolescents, at least of the male variety, the only variety with which I am really familiar, frequently appear not to be listening when they really are. Scholars tell us that Shakespeare's great theme is the contrast between appearance and reality. Teenage boys are well-acquainted with that theme. They are great at putting on appearances which are not reflective of the reality inside them. Since they do listen, we adults need to be careful what we say to them. Are we planting in their brains things which will ultimately help them to become better men or are we putting things in their heads which will lead them to become less than they could be?

When I was first operated on for colon cancer in March of 2006, I woke up to find myself surrounded by flowers. Now, most people would be delighted that so many people were so thoughtful, but not me. There were so many flowers, I felt as if I were being laid out in Witzke's funeral home. I told Mr. Fitz to tell people please not to send any more flowers. He announced to the faculty that the curmudgeon didn't want flowers! During my recovery I began to reflect on why the flowers angered me and, as I reflected, I began to realize that it was because I felt obligated to write thank-you notes for them. Feeling as poorly as I did, the thought of having to write thank-you notes just upset me. Our General Superior at the time, Brother Arthur Caliman, told me that I didn't have to worry about thank-you notes and that people would understand that, having just received a diagnosis of cancer, I was in no condition to write notes. No matter what Brother Arthur told me, from beyond the grave I heard my mother saying, "Cancer is no excuse for being impolite. When you receive a gift, you write a thank-you note." Although my mother died long before the days of e-mail, I also know that she would never approve of an e-mail thank-you note. Even a typed one wouldn't do. Thank-you notes are most properly hand-written.

On any number of occasions in my career, I have had to confront students about prejudice, and that is never an easy task because very frequently the prejudice comes from their parents. Please understand that I am not claiming to be completely free of prejudice, nor am I claiming that my parents raised me perfectly. I am probably no better or worse than most school teachers or most parents when it comes to saying the wrong thing. None of us are perfect. Nevertheless, given the influence we have over young minds, we need to be careful. Prejudices of every sort are passed down from generation to generation. I have never been a strong proponent of unions, even teacher unions, and I know that I get that from my Dad who was the head of large hospitals where he was always having union difficulties. At least I know where my attitudes come from, which can be helpful in reassessing them in light of my own adult experience.

I did write the thank-you notes. My mother has been dead for twenty-eight years, but she still influences what I do and how I think. My mother was an incredibly kind and hospitable woman, and I can see shades of the best of her both in my sister and me. Some Brothers complain that, when it's my night to cook, I cook too much. My sister always says that you can never have too many potatoes. That's Ma! My dad was wont to observe, as we sat down to eat, "Patton's army isn't coming to dinner, dear." So, you see, writing thank-you notes was only one of many things I learned from my mother, most of which had to do with making others happy.

You may not want to think about death just yet, but long after you're dust, you will still be influencing what your son does and how he thinks. What an awesome responsibility!

"What do you leave to your child when you're dead? Only whatever you put in its head. Careful the things you say. Children will listen."

On Some Aspects of the Nature of the Teenage Male

I have always felt that you can't simply dismiss male adolescent behavior with the old adage, "Boys will be boys," yet try as we might, parents and teachers, we cannot change the nature of teenage boys. We can only try to contain that nature and channel it, as best we can, in proper directions. Many things have changed since I started teaching in 1971, most notably the family structure from which our students come. Yet in all those years, I've not seen any real change in the nature of boys. They are what they are: surprising, exhilarating, exasperating, lovable, and frustrating.

Years ago, a father dragged his son into my office, yelling, "You tell the Brother what you did. I'm ashamed of you, ashamed of you." The boy, as it turned out, had been caught shoplifting. His father was mortified, but I found myself thinking, "So what's new? Tell me something new." I calmed the father down, took the boy on for a fare-thee-well and sent them both on their way. That boy went on to become vice-president of the student council and a military officer. Recently, we have had a rash of thievery at the Mount. I have been very clear and very blunt with the student body on my feelings about this. Of course, in a school of 1050 boys, there are bound to be some bad apples, and they are not always obvious. Bad apples notwithstanding, I have discovered over the years that most of the time when things are stolen, it is because the other students put temptation in the way of the bad apple. They don't lock their lockers. They leave books, jackets, sneakers, iPods, and calculators lying around everywhere and expect them to be there when they return. Thievery shouldn't happen in a Catholic school. No student in this school could deny that Mr. Fitz and I have been very clear on how we feel about such thievery. Yet, it has happened in every school with which I have been associated. A school is an imperfect place, and we have many imperfect boys here. If we only admitted perfect boys, boys who could be president of the Saint Dominic Savio Club, we really would not have any reason to exist. We're here to help imperfect boys become mature men. In addition, a school full of perfect boys would be incredibly boring. I must admit I rather enjoy working with some of our rapscallions and always have. It's part of the Xaverian charism in education always to pay attention to the underdogs and rapscallions.

Greg McDivitt '88 of our science department spoke at our Annual Father-Son Communion Breakfast and, in his address, he made it quite clear that he has been carefully watching "boy nature" for the seventeen years he has taught at the Mount. He spoke of the fact that women frequently don't understand that, when men insult and deride each other, they are quite possibly exhibiting affection. All you have to do is spend a day at Mount Saint Joseph to verify that fact. The kids are constantly dumping on each other, insulting each other, and questioning each other's legitimacy and virility. And it's all among friends! Apart from the insults, if you spent a day at the Mount, you would also think that no boy in the school has a first name. If a kid doesn't have a peer-invented nickname, he is called by his last name. "Hey, Smith, what's the homework for Kenyon?" I was at an alumni reception for the Class of 1941 not long ago. When one of the men of that class arrived late, everyone yelled together, "Here's Stinky!" The gentleman said to me, "Brother, nobody has called me Stinky since the day I graduated from the Mount." Stinky was greeted with great affection by his classmates. I don't know if he hadn't yet discovered the use of deodorant when he was a student at the Mount, but as far as his classmates were concerned, he was still Stinky.

During one of my Monday Morning Pep Talks last month, I told the students about an article in the *Baltimore Sun* concerning helicopter parents, those parents who feel they have to fly in and rescue their sons from whatever is making them unhappy. I told them that they need to learn how to fight their own battles and not to employ their parents to fight them. I was very fortunate to grow up with a father who was the direct antithesis of the helicopter parent. On the two occasions that I found myself in trouble in high school, once academically and once in a matter of discipline, my father absolutely refused to get involved. He told me, "You got yourself into it. You get yourself out of it." On both occasions I did, and it was a life lesson I have never forgotten.

In writing this letter, I know that the boys will continue to be careless with their possessions, thieves will continue to take advantage of that, and helicopter parents will continue to descend. Although I recognize all this, I still love what I do and hope that, in some small way, I'll help to make one boy more responsible with his possessions, one thief repentant, and one parent determined to let his or her son fight his own battles. It's the small victories that count.

On Things We'd Rather Forget

Years ago, while I was visiting the home of a distinguished alumnus of Saint Xavier High School who had a son in the school, the son complained to me that Dad wasn't completely pleased with the son's very respectable report card. I looked at Dad and threatened to show his high school transcript to his son. The son smiled. Dad squirmed.

During this school year, there are approximately 120 sons of Mount alumni in the student body. Now, let's suppose that I decide to have a "Let's look at your father's high school transcript" day during which I let all the sons of the Mount alumni in the present student body look at their father's high school transcripts. I suspect that there are many fathers of Mount students who would very much prefer that their sons never see Dad's high school transcript. What would happen to all those "you can do better" and "when I was your age" lectures? While there are probably many fathers who would not be at all ashamed of their high school transcripts, I would wager that they are not the majority. There were perhaps as many unrealized potentials at the Mount twenty, twenty-five and thirty years ago as there are today. It's amazing how many incredibly successful Mount alumni did not have stellar high school records. Teenage boys have a way of growing up and landing on their feet. That is true now just as it was back in the golden years when Dad attended the Mount.

Even surrounded every day by 1,050 boys, I can forget how difficult it was to be a teenager, and I suspect that the same is true for you. If I had a son, I would not want this hypothetical son to see the report card from my freshman year in high school. While it didn't end badly, it began miserably with failures in Latin and Religion. I wouldn't want this hypothetical son to see the disciplinary record from my sophomore year during which I tangled with the redoubtable Sister Mary Seretina. I picked the wrong teacher for a bit of sophomore back-talk! Sister Mary Seretina won that skirmish, and I retreated with my tail between my legs, with 30 hours of detention. Being a sophomore wasn't any easier in 1962 than it is today. Ironically, I can count on the fact that I'm going to lose my temper two or three times a year, inevitably with a sophomore who has spoken to me in a surly tone or who has given me the "you poor, pitiful adult, how dare you correct me?" look which sophomores love to give adults and which drives me crazy. I find it discouraging that, after all these years, I haven't learned how to handle these things as calmly as Sister Seretina did. She nailed me to the wall without ever raising her voice. Maybe it was the name. Seretina is Latin for serene.

Not to worry! I will not be holding a "Let's look at Dad's high school transcript" day. I know that every parent, be that parent father or mother, wants to forget some part of their own adolescence. Remember that the next time your son is being very adolescent. It just might help you to be a bit more patient.

On Getting Involved

Perhaps because I'd had a very busy summer with a long-delayed vacation to Alaska and with a trip with the General Council of the Xaverian Brothers to visit our Brothers in Kenya, I found myself in mid-August not as enthusiastic as I would like to have been about the beginning of the new school year. I had just returned from a one-day trip to Boston for a series of meetings at Malden Catholic High School, and, tuckered-out from that, I sat at my desk wondering where the energy would come for a new school year. Seeing the football team at practice on our beautiful new field, I decided to take a walk across the bridge to watch practice. I must admit I became more exhilarated just at the sight of our beautiful new field and stadium. As I wandered about the field and through the various groups practicing, the kids who noticed me waved and said, "Hi, Brother!" That was all it took. My energy started to return, and I remembered what Mr. Fitz always says, that school is not really school in the summer since the students aren't here. As I watched the kids practice, I felt the joy returning.

That very same day I encountered a boy who had just been cut from another team and, from long experience, I knew that there was very little I could say to console him. I did, however, give it my best effort, telling him to find something else and become involved. "Can you run? How about cross country? Do something!" I doubt I made much of an impression, but as I walked away from him, I thought about Rocco. A brilliant young man who graduated from MIT, Rocco was a student of mine at Saint X. For four years, Rocco ran cross county, always coming in last. He used to joke about it, telling me, "When you see me, Brother, the race is over." His poor results never bothered Rocco. Knowing that the school didn't cut anyone from cross country, he was just happy to be part of a team, doing his best and plugging along.

During his time at Mount Saint Joseph, your son may be cut from teams or not win the leading role in the school play. Your job is to help him see that minor setbacks (and being cut from a team is a minor setback!) are part of life and that he can learn from them. But above all, encourage him to become involved in something else at the Mount. I tell the kids all the time that they should not be an eight to two-thirty student. Mount Saint Joseph never closes as far as I can tell. At times it seems to me that we have students and teachers here 24/7. We have more clubs and activities than I can name, and some I can't name because we always seem to be adding to the list. Mr. Fitz is always open to student suggestions about more clubs and activities. Don't let your son sit in a corner and pout because he was cut from the tiddlywinks team. God may have closed a door, but somewhere He has opened a window. Help your son to find it!

In high school I was the classic non-jock and, given the fact that my high school did not have much besides sports, I went home every day at three o'clock until the athletic director, Father Shea, convinced me to become one of the managers of the football team. I had such a great time doing that, I became the manager of the baseball team as well. I didn't know a hit from an error, but I learned to keep score and do whatever else was necessary. I learned skills that have stood me in very good stead over the course of my life. I couldn't be one of the jocks, but I learned how to organize them. More importantly, I was able to meet kids outside of my circle whom I would never have met otherwise and coaches who became real role models for me.

There is an extracurricular activity at the Mount for your son. His experience will be much richer if he finds something with which he can become involved. We proclaim very loudly and boldly that the Mount is a community where "enduring personal relationships" are central to a Xaverian education. Extracurricular activities help to build the school community, a community in which you want your son to be fully involved. And you want to be fully involved as well. The Mothers' Club, the Fathers' Club and the Alumni Association (if you are an alumnus) always need help. Sign up!

Remember Rocco! It doesn't make any difference if your son comes in last or if he is one of the boys in the back row of the chorus in the school play whom Mrs. Esserwein encourages to sing softly. Involvement is the key! Help your son to make the Mount his second home. Help him to make memories which will warm his old age and yours.

On Giving Good Example

A few years ago, I completely lost my temper with a teacher who did not deserve the treatment I was giving him. To make matters worse, I lost my temper with the teacher within hearing range of students. As soon as it was over, I had one of those moments that we all have when we have royally fouled up: "Oh, my God, what have I done?" I immediately chased after the teacher to apologize for my very poor behavior and to apologize to him in front of the boys who had heard our interaction. I wanted them to know that I had behaved badly, that the teacher was not at fault and that I had given them very poor example. As I walked back to my office, I thought to myself, with all of my experience and after all of these years, how could I have let myself behave like that and, to make matters worse, in front of the boys? In the court of my own mind, there were no excuses I could offer. But as my novice master, Brother Kevin, used to tell us, there is no humility without humiliation. I had humiliated myself.

We adults have the awesome responsibility of giving good example to the young. As you are well aware, when you are dealing with a teenager, there has to be congruence between your words and your actions. They will point out what they see as hypocrisy in a minute. We adults have to "walk the talk" if we are going to have any influence with teenagers. Of course, only God is perfect, and we aren't. We are going to fail, on occasion, and on those occasions, I really think we need to acknowledge our failure to our sons and students so that they learn how an adult should react when he or she has not "walked the talk."

Let me give you a practical example. Once long ago in a school far away, the secretary for the prefect of discipline wrote to me: "One of the most difficult aspects I encounter in my position here is writing 'excused passes' for students who bring notes from home wherein the parent has blatantly lied about why the student was late to school or absent the day before. 'Johnny was not feeling well this morning, and that is why he is late' might actually mean that 'Johnny couldn't get his lazy butt out of bed this morning and that's why he's late'."

I had to laugh at that because, in my long experience as a school teacher and a school administrator, I know that the secretary was telling the truth. While most parents won't lie for their sons, I, unfortunately, can't enumerate the number of times in my career I have caught parents doing just that. Who can ever forget the 100 parents who wrote lies for their sons after a senior skip day in 1985, not knowing we already had names and pictures of the boys at the beach on that fateful day? I was not a very popular principal with the senior parents when I made them write a note admitting they had lied for their son before I readmitted him to school. That was silly on my part. Making the point wasn't worth the grief! Obviously, lying for your son gives him a very bad example. You, as an adult, are teaching him not to face up to his responsibility. That's not a good lesson for a teenage boy to learn. If he can't get his "lazy butt" out of bed in the morning, let him go to JUG for a few afternoons, and he'll be on time.

I have failed enough times in my life and in my career to

understand that dealing with teenage boys is not an easy thing to do. They can drive you to absolute distraction. When I have failed, I learned long ago that my job is to recognize the failure and make amends as quickly as possible. I have apologized to students, to teachers and even to the whole school, on occasions. Patience was not one of my strongest suits in my early days as a principal. Of course, I was flying by the seat of my pants and had not a clue what I was doing. You might feel that way some days about parenting.

As parents and teachers, let's all make the resolution that we are going to do our best to give the best example we can to the young men of Mount Saint Joseph. They deserve no less from us.

An Autumnal Reflection

At the Mother-Son Communion Breakfast held the day after Willie Staso '07 died, we prayed for Willie and his family. Mrs. Beth Czyryca of our faculty was there with her son and, when she heard that Willie had died, she obviously became quite upset. I asked her, "Is he the first former student of yours to die?" Of course, I knew the answer. I also knew that I couldn't count the number of my former students who have died, nor can I remember all the details and the circumstances. There have simply been far too many. Somebody asked me not long ago if I had ever had a student commit suicide while the boy was in school. I replied that I hadn't. At that, Brother Bob Flaherty said to me, "How could you forget the boy at Saint X when we were both stationed there?" How could I? It was absolutely dreadful. Perhaps as a defense mechanism, I've blotted out a lot of the details. I do remember this much. During the nine years that I was principal at Xavier High School in Middletown, Connecticut, nine boys died, three in one year. In those nine years, not one girl at Mercy High School, our sister school down the road, died. Now, some of those boys died in accidents that were not at all their fault, and one, as far as I can remember, died of natural causes. The rest were involved in risky behavior with fatal consequences.

What is it about boys that makes them prone to such risk taking? I have read that the male brain develops later, and that the area of the brain which controls judgment is one of the last things to develop. I'm no scientist, so I don't know how true that is. It certainly sounds plausible. That boys mature later than girls I do know as an absolute fact. I have been watching it for thirty-seven years. I've even seen it in younger members of the faculties over which I have presided. Young women teachers seem to approach the business of school more seriously and more quickly than their male counterparts. There is still a little bit of the "college boy" in some young male teachers. Of course, I'm not talking about Mount Saint Joseph! These things happened in schools long ago and far away.

So how do we talk to our sons and our students about avoiding risky behavior without sounding like cranky adults who are simply on their case? I honestly don't know. There are times when I have just settled on being the cranky adult. The thing I don't know—and won't know this side of heaven—is how many times they have listened and have been saved from themselves and from tragedy because they did listen. You and I only see the sad examples of the ones who didn't. Maybe in God's provident love there are a host of them who actually have listened even when they pretended that we were just talking nonsense.

Keep talking to your sons, trying to find the best way to communicate. Yes, he'll roll his eyes. Yes, he'll complain. But if you find a way to do it so that he understands it's because you love him very dearly, maybe he actually will listen. It's worth a try and is certainly far better than the alternative. Even as I write this, I am reminded of how many times I have written the same thing in the past.

November is the month of "howling winds and holy souls," and these rather somber reflections probably fit the month.

I have a profound faith in my vocation as a Brother, having learned long ago to live with the pain of not having children of my own. Being celibate, I can never know or understand fully the grief of parents who have lost a child. Only parents who have lost a child can understand that. Nevertheless, this old Brother long ago tired of teenage funerals, yet they continue to happen. Let's work together to impress on our sons and our students not only the promise of life, but its fragility as well. We owe them that!

On Differing Perspectives

I recently joined the Board of Trustees for my alma mater, Marian High School, in Framingham, Massachusetts. While I don't need any more work or board obligations, I wanted to help Marian as a sign of my gratitude to the Sisters of Saint Joseph of Boston who taught me at the school and who helped to shape the student and the teacher I have become. When I attended the school from 1961 until 1965, the faculty was almost entirely composed of Sisters of Saint Joseph. Now the principal, Sister Catherine Clifford, is the only Sister of Saint Joseph on the staff. The school has struggled with enrollment in recent years, and Sister Cathy has worked mightily to maintain the spirit of the Sisters of Saint Joseph who began the school in 1956 and set its firm foundations. In my office at Mount Saint Joseph, I have pictures of three Sisters of Saint Joseph who taught me: Sister Anna Catherine Ford, Sister Miriam Patricia McLeod and Sister Mary Denisita White. All three women had an integral part in helping to form the man I have become.

When I mentioned that I had a picture of Sister Anna Catherine in my office, Sister Cathy told me that she recently received a phone call from an alumnus who said that he would give nothing to Marian High School because his memories of Sister Anna Catherine were not very pleasant. I suppose I can understand, to some degree, his perspective. Sister Anna

Catherine was relentless when it came to damming the flood of human foolishness. She was the mortal enemy of Peter Pan. Boys in her class who did not want to grow up were given very short shrift. I know because I was one of them. She took me, a very intelligent but incredibly lazy boy, and molded me into a student who was eager to learn. Because she never let me or anyone else off the hook, I learned that if I did my work, I could learn and could actually enjoy learning. It took failures in Latin and religion in the first marking period to get my attention, but get my attention she did. She also got my father's attention! Once I discovered that, with effort, I could do the work, even when she piled on one hundred word problems in Algebra over the winter vacation, school wasn't so bad. She may have scared me at first, but she taught me my potential and made me want to actualize it. I came to love school and learning, even when the work was difficult. I came to rejoice in intellectual challenges, all because of a woman whom one of my contemporaries apparently found a stumbling block. He won't give a dime to Marian High School because of her, and because of her, I'm giving Marian High School time that I really don't have. It's amazing how different perspectives can be!

In the tradition of Sister Anna Catherine, I have very little patience with Peter Pan, and I suppose there are some men, over the course of my career, who found me more of a nemesis than a salvation. I hope they are in the minority, but I'm glad I won't find that out until heaven. Then it won't matter!

Thank God that schools and faculties are diverse. One boy's nemesis as a teacher is another boy's salvation. Fortunately, we have so many mission-minded teachers at the Mount that every boy should be able to find salvation with at least one of them, if not most. When kids complain to me that a teacher is tough, I use the old cliché, "When the going gets tough, the tough get going. Stop whining and do your work. You might actually discover that you like it."

The day that Sister Cathy and I had the discussion about Sister Anna Catherine, I took some time to visit Sister Mary Campion, my math teacher in senior year, who is eighty-six years old and who lives in the infirmary of the Sisters of Saint Joseph in Framingham. A nurse was pushing her out of a room in a wheelchair, and I recognized her immediately by her angelic smile, which I remembered vividly. When I told her who I was, she smiled that beautiful smile and said, "It is sweet of you to come see me, dear, but I have absolutely no recollection of you." Just another lesson in humility! Of course, the important thing is not that she remembers me, but that I remember her.

Every year, a steady stream of Mount alumni visit the school to see the teachers who were important to them and to express, in their own stumbling ways, their gratitude for what was done for them here. I've even seen alumni thank a teacher who was his nemesis! Perspectives do change.

On Haircuts and Adolescent Rebellion

Long ago in a school far away, there was a boy who refused to have his hair cut. He worked his way through the chain of command until he landed in my office. Unaware just how deep his adolescent rebellion was running, I smiled, told him not to be silly, and to have his hair cut. He adamantly refused. Confronted with this obstinacy, I told him to bring his father in to see me the next day. The father, defending his son, told me that I was violating his son's constitutional rights. Trained as I was by the great Catholic school legal guru, Sister Mary Angela Shaughnessy, I pointed out that his son had no constitutional rights in a Catholic school, that his son's rights came from contract law. Part of the contract was the school handbook, which both he and his son had signed and which stated how his son's hair was to be cut. A relentless force had hit an immovable object, and as far as I can remember, he withdrew his son from school.

Not long ago, we had a similar hair problem at Mount Saint Joseph. The father wanted his son to cut his hair, but the son wouldn't. After the boy and his father left the office, Mr. Fitz and I both speculated on what would have happened forty-five years ago if either of us had told our Irish fathers that we wouldn't have our hair cut. Neither of us could imagine defying our fathers—point-blank—like that. It just didn't happen, at least not in our Irish families in those days long ago.

All teenage boys go through a rebellious streak as they try to find their way into manhood. Most of the time, the rebellion is not terribly serious, but at other times it can be quite serious. When confronted with a rebellious teenage boy, I usually start by coaxing and cajoling, trying to bring him around to my way of thinking. Failing that, I become coldly logical. Teenage boys can become quickly irrational when their divine wills are being thwarted, and I discovered long ago that the worst thing I can do is become irrational along with them. I try to stay calm, collected and logical, meeting the rebellion point for point. Mind you, I have had plenty of occasions when I have violated my own rule. If you haven't noticed, teenage boys can drive you to distraction pretty easily.

It is a part of the very essence of a teenage boy to test the limits. That's how he comes to understand proper boundaries. As his parents, you need to decide how far you will let him go as he tests you. You need to be flexible here. He has to have some victories in the battle (and if you haven't noticed yet, it really is a battle!). You are his parents, and as long as you are paying the bills, he needs to abide by your rules. Give him some leeway, but be firm and consistent in those matters which you have decided are non-negotiable. Some boys, certainly not the majority, can go overboard with adolescent rebellion, making everyone's life miserable. In those instances, I usually recommend that parents contact our guidance counselors for help with how to proceed. I joke with Mr. Belzner that, in the old days, the Brothers used to refer to Guidance as the "elephants' graveyard," because it was where old Brothers went when their teaching days were over. Those days have long since passed, and our Guidance Department is an incredibly professional group of men and women who are there to help you as you confront the challenges of raising a teenage boy.

One last story! In the same school, far away and long ago, another young man refused to have his hair cut. Confronted as he was with an ultimatum, the clever lad decided to bobby pin the offending locks under his hair so that it appeared he had gotten a haircut. Everyone was happy until the bobby pin let loose during class. He was immediately dispatched to the dean of students. Further rebellion landed him in my office. I told him that he had two options. He could get his hair cut or he could return with his parents on Monday with signed withdrawal papers. On Monday he appeared in my office and showed me that the offending locks were gone and that his hair was properly cut and not booby-trapped. I smiled and complimented him on his common sense. As he was leaving, he told me he had a present for me. Wrapped in tissue paper were the offending locks. He said that, since the school was so obsessed with his hair, he thought that I should have the locks as a memento. I smiled. He went back to class, and the offending locks went into the waste basket. I gave a quiet sigh of relief and went on to the next problem of the day.

Don't be surprised by adolescent rebellion. It is part and parcel of the journey from boy to man. If coaxing and cajoling fail, be coldly logical. Try to stay calm when he's doing his best to push you into an irrational outburst. Failing all of that, quite calmly send him to his room until he's thirty!

On Boys as Barometers

No schoolteacher ever prays for an early spring in an all-boys' school because boys are human barometers. As the sap begins to rise in the trees and as the buds begin to bloom, so do the spirits of the 1050 boys here at the Mount. Having seen this now in four different schools, I can attest that it is not just a Mount phenomenon; it is an all-boys' phenomenon. The noise level in a boys' school is always a low rumble. There is nothing high-pitched about it as I might imagine there is in a girls' school. But as spring advances and the sap rises, the low rumble begins to increase in decibels. The freshmen on their way to gym at the beginning of the eighth period are particularly noisy. As I look out my window, they are pushing and shoving playfully, laughing and joking and taking their sweet time arriving for gym class.

Pushing and shoving! That increases with the spring. As I walked from my classroom back to the office this morning, at least six times I told kids to stop pushing and shoving. They really weren't doing anything wrong. They were just being frisky, but in the spring when friskiness increases, so do the occasional fights. These are always fights between good friends when the pushing and shoving escalates a bit too far. Of course, since they are boys, they forget about it as soon as it is over and become friends again. I just resign myself to the fact that I will add, "Stop shoving" to my normal repertoire of "Tuck your shirt in and put your tie up." The exuberance that comes to boys in spring is, in many ways, refreshing after a long, gray Maryland winter. It can, however, try the patience of teachers who are attempting to reach the end of their syllabi.

With spring, the ordinarily short attention span of a boy becomes almost non-existent. I had a chat this morning with one of my best students who handed me an incredibly poor essay. His work is normally so good that I save his essays for last so that I can end on a high note. He could give me no reasonable explanation as to why he did not give me his normally stellar performance, but I knew why. Spring! I trust that our little chat knocked him back into winter for a while. The old adage, "In spring a young man's fancy turns to thoughts of love," definitely has some truth to it. Adolescent love blossoms in the spring. Of course, adolescent love can be pretty fickle. The girl he so proudly brought to the Junior Prom may only be a dim memory by the time the Senior Prom rolls around; however, that is not always true. Nothing is always true when it comes to teenage boys. I just received an invitation to the wedding of a former student who is marrying the girl he introduced to me at his Junior Prom.

As in school, so at home. I suspect that you see some changes in your son in the spring of the year. There really is something refreshing about all of that enthusiasm, but, enthusiasm notwithstanding, I have always agreed with Brother Frederick who walked into the community room at Saint John's High School on one beautiful spring day and announced to the assembled Brothers, "It's time for the school year to be over and the boys to be gone." We all said, "Amen!"

Spring is my favorite time of the year in school. I love wandering the campus, watching games and practices, and seeing all of that boyish exuberance put to good use on the playing fields. The spirit of a boys' school is something unique and very refreshing. While I very much enjoyed my own experience in a coeducational high school forty-five years ago, there are times when I wish that I'd had the experience that the young men at the Mount are having now. As one young man said to me the other day, "It's good to be a Mount man."

On Churchill and Expectations

Recently during my never-ending study of Winston Churchill, I came upon two quotes which struck a resonating chord within me. The first is, "A woman is as old as she looks. A man is as old as he feels, and a boy is as old as he is treated." The second, "Success is never final, and failure is never fatal. It's courage that counts."

"A boy is as old as he is treated." That has to be put in the context of the Battle of Britain at the beginning of the Second World War. If the Royal Air Force were unable to defeat the Luftwaffe, Britain would have lost the war in its first days. Many of the pilot officers of the Royal Air Force were mere boys, eighteen- and nineteen-year-olds, who had been given a death-defying task. Britain needed them to be men, treated them as men, and they acted as men. They might have become boys again when they were on leave and hit the nightlife of London, but when they were on duty, they were men.

It has been my personal observation—and it could be quite wrong—but I have noticed in recent years that it takes longer for young men to grow up and become responsible than it did when I was younger. I've seen this in young teachers and in young alumni. The "college-boy syndrome" seems to last past college. I wonder if this is because we don't expect enough of them. We are so concerned with stroking their egos and making them feel good about themselves that perhaps we don't sufficiently challenge them to grow up and become the men God wants them to be. I see this in myself as a teacher, and I consider myself a fairly rigorous teacher. I am, however, nowhere near as rigorous as I was twenty years ago. It goes hand-in-hand with the "dumbing down" of text books. I'm not being cranky here. It's just fact. As I think about the boys at the Mount (and I do think of them as boys), I wonder if we are expecting as much of them as we should. Are we teaching them, by high expectations, to become the men we hope they will be? We say that we are building men who matter at the Mount, and I honestly believe that we are doing that. My question is: could we do it better and more rigorously? This isn't just a question for teachers at the Mount. It's a question for you as parents. How high are your expectations? My sister once opined that our parents, because they were older when they had children, just expected us to act like adults. As I look back at my upbringing, I can see some truth in that. My father was never afraid to let me know how he expected me to behave. He expected me to become a good student, and he was relentless in letting me know that he would tolerate nothing less. Figuratively chained to the dining room table every day after school until he came home, I learned to do homework and to do it well.

"Success is never final, and failure is never fatal. It's courage that counts." Churchill's second quote is related to the first. Success is certainly ephemeral. Witness the current economy and the loss of jobs of many successful people. If success is a value, it is a value which must be cultivated continually and always in the context of the transitory nature of life. "We have here no lasting city," as St. Paul writes in his letter to the Hebrews. In the ebb and flow of my own life, I am often struck

by this fact. Before I came to Mount Saint Joseph, I was head of two other large Xaverian Brothers high schools. During my years at those schools, I think I was a rather successful Headmaster. At both schools, I am nothing but a very dim memory now. My success at those schools is a dim memory, but so are my failures. *"Failure is never fatal."* That's a truth I have tried to pound into the heads of wondering school boys for the last thirty years. A boy can learn far more from his failures than he can from his successes. Those failures can bring him to Churchill's last point, *"It's courage that counts."* If we hold our boys to high expectations, and if we teach them to learn from their failures, we will inculcate in them the virtue of courage. If we give them a humble and healthy attitude toward success, they will realize that it is, in fact, courage which counts.

Does all of this seem paradoxical? Is it paradoxical to hold them to high expectations, but teach them not to be afraid of failure and to be wary of success? Certainly it is! But the entire Christian message is paradoxical. The first shall be last. If you would save your life, you must first lose it. To bear fruit, the seed must die. Jesus certainly knew paradox.

How can I sum this all up? Expect the best from your son. Don't let him settle for less than the best. Support him when he fails, but help him to learn from his failure. Teach him that courage is what ultimately matters.

More on Motivation

Every year on the feast of St. Thomas More, I e-mail many of my former students to remind them of the play *A Man for All Seasons* which they read with me during their junior year in high school. St. Thomas More was a man who put his faith in God before his loyalty to King Henry VIII and died for it. In the play, his daughter, Margaret, comes to him in prison and says to her father, "Haven't you done all that God can reasonably want?" To this, Thomas More replies, "Well, finally, it isn't a matter of reason. Finally, it is a matter of love." Thomas More's faith is not disembodied. His faith is intimately bound up with his profound love of God, and while people of the time thought that he was dying for his principles, he was, in fact, dying because he could not violate the loving relationship which he had with his God. In reality, his final words to the headsman on the scaffold were, "I die his majesty's good servant, but God's first."

I write to my old boys on the feast of St. Thomas More to remind them all of this. In a previous letter, I've written to you about motivation, and admitted that the teacher in me never wants to give up. Many of my "old boys" are now well over fifty years old, but I'm still trying to motivate them. The result of this annual e-mail always gives me hope—hope that men I taught two, twenty-two, and thirty-two years ago might still be profiting from what I taught them.

I begin every school year by telling my English class that what I am about to teach them will make much more sense to them when they are in their thirties and forties. Literature, and poetry, in particular, demands experience. A sonnet by Shakespeare about lost love will be purely an academic exercise for my students until they've been dumped in a ditch by Molly Mt. de Sales or Sally Seton Keough or Nancy Notre Dame. Then the poem will come to life. Of course, when I point this out to them, they smile smugly as if to insist that will never happen to them. We expose them to great literature when they are young, hoping that they will remember some of it as life brings them new and varied experiences.

After this year's e-mail on the feast of St. Thomas More, I received the following reply from David Trier, a young man whom I taught in the late 1990s and who is now an engineer, having graduated from the University of Notre Dame:

> Thanks, Brother James and yes, my mother is ready for grandchildren. By the way, after you sent this e-mail, I went back to my book collection and picked up *A Man for All Seasons*. I thoroughly enjoyed it the second time around. In fact, I still have all the books from your class. I've just started *The Razor's Edge* after finishing with St. Thomas More. It's funny how much more appreciation you have for these classics after more life experiences and general maturation.

Well, as you can imagine, that warmed the cockles of this old teacher's heart. And I think there is a lesson here for parents as well as old teachers. Teenage boys may appear not to pay attention to anything we are saying. In fact, at times they go out of their way to let us know that they consider us either old-fashioned or out of touch or completely lacking in any understanding of their life situation. At times, they revel in letting us know just how "out of it" we are. One of our teachers once told me that he had decided that a teenage daughter considers it her job to let her father know every day just how stupid he is! That holds true for teenage sons as well. Yet, despite appearances to the contrary, they are listening, and they are taking in all that we are trying to teach them. At this point in their lives, they can't let us know that. It would be a betrayal of their teenage honor. But they are listening. Every day, you are teaching your son the values you want him to hold in life. Every day, you are teaching him how to be a good parent when the time comes. He is paying very careful attention, even on those days when his mind seems a million miles away. That's why we adults have to be so careful in our interactions with the young. They'll pick up the bad as well as the good. When I think about some of my worst days in the classroom over the last thirty-eight years, I worry about the bad example I may have given. Fortunately, the good days far outnumber the bad.

Remember the words of Thomas More's profound reply: "Finally it isn't a matter of reason. Finally it's a matter of love." Have confidence that your love for your son will ultimately be what he remembers and will ultimately help to motivate him to become the man God wants him to be. Remember this particularly on those days when he appears to be letting you know how stupid you are!

In Praise of Praise

Over the years, I have noticed that, whenever you praise a boy to his mother, she beams with pride, thanks you effusively, and frequently tears up. When you praise a boy to his father, the father blusters, looks embarrassed, and suggests that the boy is more of a screw-up than you know. Both reactions always make me smile. Since I rarely have the occasion to praise girls to their mothers or fathers, I don't know if the reaction is reversed, but I suspect it might be. I've mentioned before the old Irish joke asking the question, "How do you know that Jesus is Irish?" The answer is that his mother thought he was God. A little Catholic humor there!

Fathers are very concerned that their sons grow up as men who can handle themselves in the world and, probably for that reason, they tend to be a bit harder in judging them. That doesn't mean that they love their sons any less. Mothers have an entirely different perspective. Not long ago, I was speaking with the adult son of a friend of mine, and I commented to him that his father had an incredible wit. The son replied, "Tell me about it! I've borne the brunt of my father's wit all my life." He didn't say that angrily, but more with calm resignation. Shortly after that, his father introduced me to his daughter on whom he obviously doted. I picked up on the father-son, father-daughter dynamic immediately.

My own father rarely praised me to my face. I think if he was happy with me, he told my sister. He always praised my sister to me. Mr. Fitz wrote a few months ago that he didn't have the blessing of a sister. I, most fortunately, have that blessing. Many times I have said to the Brothers in my community who are only children that they lack the one essential thing for taking care of elderly parents, a sister. My sister took beautiful care of our father until the day he died. Of course, that's not the only blessing of having a sister! I know that my father was very proud of me, but it was not part of his upbringing to say so. Even when I was an adult and head of a school, my father felt that there were little adjustments he needed still to make in my personality. For example, he always told me that I didn't shave closely enough. During his days as a professional businessman, he was always impeccably dressed and immaculately groomed. I think he saw it as blight on the family honor that I wasn't quite as impeccable or as immaculate.

What is the point of all this? Well, I don't think we're going to change family dynamics which seem ingrained in the human psyche, but it is good occasionally for fathers to remember how important it is to praise their son. It's amazing what a little praise will do for a teenage boy. When I first came to Mount Saint Joseph in 2001, a man whom I had taught in the 1970s saw the announcement of my appointment in the paper and brought his family to the Mount to meet me. As he was leaving, he said to me, "No one praised me much in my education, but I remember one day when you praised me in front of the class for something I had written. I have never forgotten that." I had absolutely no memory of that moment, but it obviously had an effect on the man that has lasted for over thirty years.

A little praise can go a long way. No doubt you chide your

son enough, and he probably needs that chiding. Just remember to balance it with praise when he shows the slightest sign of doing something well. Your son will grow into the man you hope he'll be. Just remember, it will be on his time table and not yours.

On God the Father and My Father

I was once on a directed retreat when my retreat director, Sister Martha, commented, "You must have had a wonderful father." When I asked her what prompted that comment, she replied, "Because you have such a beautiful image of God the Father. You could only get such a beautiful image from your own father." I had to stop and think about that. My father was one of the most brilliant men I have ever met, and he was almost completely self-educated. A voracious reader, he was never without a book, many of which he read multiple times. My father and Churchill agreed that if a book isn't worth reading twice, it wasn't worth reading once. All of this being said, however, my father was not a perfect man as I was not a perfect son. Yet somehow, my father instilled in me a confidence in him which gave me a very stable youth.

I could talk to my father about anything when I was a boy and, although he was an incredibly quiet and shy man, he always seemed to know what to say and when to say it. When I told him that I wanted to join the Brothers against his and my mother's wishes, he hesitated for about a week and then called me to his office where he signed the papers. As he signed them, he said, "If you're not a happy man twenty years from now, I won't have you blaming your mother and me for it. This is what you want, but you will have to live with the consequences of it, for good or for bad." Thirty years later, shortly before he died, he said to me, "Your mother and I thought you were being very foolish when you wanted to join the Brothers at the age of eighteen. You were far wiser than either of us. You knew what was going to make you happy, and you chose it, despite our objections." My father always told me the truth.

More than anything else, my father provided his family with stability. He was a man who was always there. Since he was the administrator of a large state hospital, we lived on the grounds. He came home every day for lunch and, like clockwork, he came home every afternoon at 5:00. He was so regular that our family dog, Gigi, went to her post on the back porch every evening at 4:55. I often wondered if the dog could tell time or if she could smell my father coming. Dad and Gigi would go for a walk; my mother and father would then have a drink, after which we sat down to dinner cooked by my mother and served by my father. My sister and I stayed at the table until Dad excused us. It was a family ritual that never varied, and it gave both my sister and me stability which I know I didn't appreciate at the time.

As we celebrate Father's Day in the month of June, it's important for fathers to realize how very important they are in the lives of their sons. A father has the awesome responsibility to teach his son what it means to be a man and to provide his son with the stability necessary to become not just a man, but the man God intends him to be. That requires time and attention on a father's part. That doesn't mean they need to share the same interest, although that can help. My father loved to fish. Fishing drove me crazy. I couldn't sit still, and my fidgetiness drove my father crazy. I think we last fished together when I was six and nearly overturned the boat on the Quabbin

Reservoir. I also think sons have a responsibility to nurture their relationships with their fathers. I developed an interest in Winston Churchill because my father was fascinated by him. Reading all that I could about Churchill gave me something I could discuss with my dad. Many men and their sons have sports as a bond. Whatever the case may be, fathers and sons need to find some common ground that they can share.

The Gospel reading for Mass on Thursday of the fifth week of Easter is the beautiful passage from Saint John where Jesus says to his disciples, "As the Father has loved me, so I have loved you. Remain in my love." The relationship between Jesus and his Father is the model for all father-son relationships. Years from now when your son has a son, you will want him to be able to say to that boy, "As my father loved me, so I love you." Indeed a father's love for—and dedication to—his son can be a beautiful reflection of the love of God our Father. Amen!

SECTION THREE

Mothers and Sons

In another story from Respecting the Man the Boy Will Become, *I describe a profound experience I had during my second year teaching, when the mother of a boy in my homeroom died, and my mentor, Brother Ivan, had me organize my homeroom so that all the boys would attend the wake and the funeral. Brother Ivan told me at the time, "Nothing is so tragic as a boy losing his mother. She's the one he counts on to love him no matter what." I drove a school bus all over Worcester County collecting the forty boys in my class, and taught them how to go through a receiving line at a wake. Being nervous, they followed my instructions to the letter, and each one said to John and to his father, "I'm sorry for your loss. I'll pray for you." When I came up trailing the end, the father said to me, "I know, Brother, you're sorry for our loss."*

It was early in my career that I learned about the special relationship between a boy and his mother. Of course, I knew that instinctively with my own mother. I think most men will agree that, in some ways, their mothers still think of them as boys, no matter how successful they have become as men.

Every year I try to write something, usually in May, about the beauty of the mother-son relationship. Brother Ivan was quite correct that a boy relies on his mother to love him no matter what, and that extends into manhood as well! Based on Brother Ivan's assertion, I felt that my letters to mothers about their sons deserved a special section in this book. I hope you agree!

On Saint Monica and a Mother's Prayer

Recently, I was perusing the catalog of *Bridge Building Images* and saw a beautiful Icon of Saint Monica, the mother of Saint Augustine. The explanation of the icon reads:

> Saint Monica was born to Christian parents in North Africa. By arrangement she married Patricius, then a pagan, who was abusive and unfaithful. Nevertheless, Monica bore three children, including Augustine. When Augustine's studies led him to Carthage, he fell away from the Church, even embraced heresy, and led a wayward life. Always embracing the Christian faith, Monica lived to see the power of God convert her husband and return her son to that faith. But first, amid many tears, Monica cast Augustine out of her home. She prayed to turn Augustine from this dissolute lifestyle. Then a comforting vision, symbolized by the angel at her ear, urged Monica to recall him, and a priest consoled her saying, "The child of those tears shall never perish." Her prayers were truly answered when Augustine came to accept instruction in the faith from Bishop Ambrose. Augustine was baptized, eventually becoming a priest, bishop and one of the greatest theologians in Church history.

Every year, beginning in February, I begin to harass the seniors, telling them frequently, "Don't do anything stupid between now and graduation that would jeopardize your graduation and break your mother's heart." It's a sad fact, but true, that boys (and men!) can do stupid things, take wrong paths and break their mother's hearts. I can't tell you how many times over the years I have had mothers say to me, "I can only pray, Brother, that he comes to his senses." I had a father once say to me about his son, "The only good thing I can think of is that his mother is not alive to see this. How it would have broken her heart." In that case, having known the mother, I was sure that, ultimately, her prayers from heaven would bring her son back to his senses.

When I was a boy growing up in Massachusetts, there was a famous priest, Father Feeney, who had been excommunicated for teaching the heresy that there is no salvation outside the Catholic Church. Poor Father Feeney had a rather narrow view of God! I remember that the nuns used to tell us that Father Feeney would be reconciled with the Church before he died, because his mother was a saintly woman who prayed for him daily. Sure enough, shortly before he died, Father Feeney was reconciled with the Church and received back into the fold by the saintly Bishop Flanagan of Worcester.

The moral of all this is: never underestimate the power of a mother's prayer for her child. A mother's prayer for her child has a special efficacy before God because, in God's plan of salvation, God has a mother. Remember the story of Jesus at the wedding feast of Cana. Mary ignores Jesus' protest, telling the wine stewards, "Do whatever He tells you." Good son that He was, Jesus did what His mother asked. I suspect that, if Christ ignored the prayers of a mother, He would get an earful from the Blessed Virgin!

Saint Augustine was not the first man, nor the last, to be

saved from folly because of his mother's prayers. If, now or in the future, your son goes astray, remember Saint Monica, break out those rosary beads or favorite prayer book and lay siege to heaven, knowing that God will never ignore the prayers of a mother for her child. The bond between mother and child is eternal, transcending even death. You knew that from the first moment that you held your son. His welfare will always be in your hands and in the power of your prayer.

Happy Mother's Day!

On Mothers and Grandmothers

I have been reflecting recently on my mother's family and on the end of my mother's generation with the deaths of my last two aunts. I would like to reflect this month on my mother and my grandmother who seem to me a very appropriate topic for May.

I didn't know my maternal grandmother well, although she died when I was sixteen. She spoke no English, and I, no French. For the last few years of her life she was lost in the clouds of Alzheimer's and was a patient in the hospital for the elderly at which my father was one of the chief administrators. We lived on the hospital grounds, and everyday my mother would go to my grandmother's room in the hospital to feed her with a baby bottle because my grandmother was incapable of eating on her own and because her body was too fragile for intravenous feeding. Being sixteen, I don't think I ever realized the emotional toll that this must have taken on my mother every day. To see her mother in such a helpless state, not recognizing her or anyone else, could not have been easy for a daughter to bear. I substituted for my mother whenever she couldn't make it and helped to feed my grandmother, but although I loved her, I didn't have a strong emotional bond. The night my grandmother died, the head nurse called my dad who told my mother. I walked into the dining room to find my mother crying in my father's arms. My dad looked at me and said, "Memere just died." I think I wondered at the time why my mother was crying, given the state that my grandmother had been in for the last few years, but, of course, I was sixteen, with all the insensitivity that teenage boys can have. My memories of my grandmother and my mother's memories of her mother were two entirely different things.

After my grandmother died, and even after my mother died, I began to hear stories which I didn't know about my mother's youth and about her family. In fact, my ignorance about both my mother's and my father's family has led me, over the years, to suggest to the students, during my Monday morning pep talk, that they talk to their grandparents about their family history, something I wish I had done when I was younger.

My mother died at the age of sixty-six, and I think that might have been because she had some very serious health problems when she was a very young girl. She had survived both diphtheria and scarlet fever. After my mother died, one of my aunts told me about my mother's diphtheria. When my mother contracted the disease, the doctor quarantined their house and told my grandparents to take their other children away. My grandfather took my mother's four sisters and brother away from the house and the disease, leaving my grandmother to nurse my mother. Before my grandfather left, he put my mother on the dining room table so that it would be easier for my grandmother to nurse her. My mother was not expected to live, but my grandmother paid no attention to that. All by herself, she stared down death and nursed her youngest daughter back to health. I suspect that those were the memories in my mother's heart when she wept in my father's arms after learning of her mother's death. Memories of a mother are incredibly deep.

When my mother died seventeen years after my grandmother, I was thirty-three and much more in touch with my mother's tears at the death of her own mother. Being a man, however, I suppressed those tears because I had a demanding job and work to do. One day, six months after my mother's death, as I was sitting in my office at Xavier High School in Connecticut looking for some papers in my desk, I came across the last birthday card my mother had sent to me. All that it took was the sight of her handwriting, and I began to cry and couldn't stop. One of the secretaries came in and asked me what was wrong. I told her to just close the door and to leave me alone. I learned that day, on a practical level, what I had learned on a theoretical level when I got my Master's degree in counseling: you can't suppress emotions. You can channel them, but you can't suppress them. Eventually they will have their say. When I recovered, the secretary, who was old enough to be my mother and who knew me pretty well, said, "You didn't give yourself time to grieve. I knew this was going to happen because you came back to school and threw yourself into work as if nothing had happened." What I didn't understand at sixteen, I understood at thirty-three—once I let myself understand it.

Sons may not always understand the memories in their mother's hearts and, at times, they can be incredibly insensitive, as I was when my grandmother died. But sons do grow up, and they learn. I always say that mothers are the preservers of a family's memories. Once your son is grown, you can be sure that he will cherish those memories and he will be grateful.

On Good Mothers and Clean Underwear

On my desk sits a mug which asks the question, "Are you wearing clean underwear?" The mug was given to me by a mother after I addressed the Mothers' Club on the timely topic of good mothers and clean underwear. I have never discussed this with my sister, so I don't know if my mother was as obsessed with my sister's underwear as she was with mine. Although my mother was French-Canadian and not Irish, she had Irish guilt down to perfection. She would say to me very frequently, "Change your underwear every day. God forbid you should have to go to the hospital wearing dirty underwear. They will think you have a bad mother. You don't want them to think you have a bad mother, do you?" Of course, I didn't want anyone to think I had a bad mother. I loved my mother. The French-Canadian/Irish guilt was her way of making sure that I changed my underwear every day. My mother had a heart attack when I was thirteen, and one night my father came to me and said, "Mrs. Becker, next door, is going to do our laundry for us, but I can't find your dirty underwear. Where is it?" I told him that it was where I always put it, under my bed. That, of course, brought forth a tirade: "No wonder your poor mother had a heart attack. You make her clean out your underwear from under your bed?" Sensitive a teenager as

I was, even I knew that my mother did not have a heart attack because I put my dirty underwear under the bed.

When I came home for my first vacation four years after I entered the Xaverian Brothers, my mother was appalled by the state of my underwear. Typical man that I was, I just washed everything together. In those days, we wore white underwear and black everything else. Washed all together, my underwear was basically a dull gray. From that moment on, my mother decided she had to adjust to the fact that I was not going to have a wife. Every year on my birthday, I would receive a huge supply of new underwear and new socks with the note, "Throw out everything I gave you last year and start using this. Wash whites and colors separately. Love, Mom."

When I was twenty-three years old, I was rushed to the hospital with a very painful kidney stone. As I was lying on a gurney, a nurse came by and said to me, "You certainly are not in very good shape." I replied, "No, I'm not, but I want you to know that I am wearing clean underwear." Without missing a beat, the nurse replied, "And that is because you have a good mother."

Things went along swimmingly in the underwear department for the next ten years until my mother died when I was thirty-three years old. A few years after that, as I was dressing for school one morning, I noticed that my underwear was pretty ratty. I wondered how that had happened. Then, of course, I realized that since Ma was dead, I had not received any new underwear since the birthday before she died. I shed a few tears and then went out and bought new underwear.

During the course of my ministry, I have discovered that it is not just mothers who are obsessed with clean underwear, but grandmothers as well. I had two boys in Connecticut whose mother had died, and their grandmother took over managing the household for her son and her grandsons. I visited them once and, on the dining room table, were piles of neatly laundered underwear. One of the boys said to me, "That's Grandma. Grandmas see to it that you wear clean underwear." Since we have a number of grandmothers who are the guardians of Mount Saint Joseph students, I suspect that holds true here as well.

I don't know if all mothers are as obsessed with clean underwear as my mother was, but I suspect they probably are, so all of us Mount men can probably say, "Happy Mother's Day, Mom. Thanks for making me wear clean underwear."

ON ETERNAL BONDS

The Church, as you well know, dedicates the month of May to our Blessed Mother and, from my pre-Vatican II boyhood, I have very fond memories of May processions and May hymns. The Blessed Virgin, as the Mother of God, is the prototype of all mothers. I have always found great significance in the fact that Jesus' last words to his beloved disciple Saint John were, "Take care of my mother." There is, indeed, something special about the mother-son relationship, and I'd like to tell a story to illustrate that, a story which some mothers have already heard since I know that I have used it at least once at the Mother-Son Communion Breakfast.

Tom's mother died at the end of his freshman year. Seriously ill for quite some time, she died at home one morning shortly after Tom had left for school. I remember so well his father coming to school to tell him of her death, and as sad as that scene was, it was also rather beautiful. Tom progressed through the grades, and when it was time for the senior Mother-Son Mass and dinner, some faculty suggested to him that he ask one of his aunts to accompany him to the celebration. He refused. "No one replaces my mother. I'll come, but I'll come alone."

The evening of the event, after the Mass, I was looking for the lovely Mrs. Karen White who was one of the faculty moderators. Since she was the most responsible and dutiful of women, I was surprised when I couldn't find her. Later in the evening I saw her, and being the insensitive man I can be, said, "Karen, where have you been?" Her reply left me ashamed of myself and very proud of her.

She said: "At the end of the Mass, Brother, I saw Tom standing at the back of the auditorium holding the rose that each boy gives to his mother. I went up to him and asked, 'Tom, what do you want to do with that rose?' He replied, 'I want you to come with me to Saint Michael's cemetery so I can give this rose to my mother.' I knew that you would want me to go with him, so I did, and we placed the rose on his mother's grave."

The point here is quite obvious, but being the teacher that I am, I have to expatiate. The bond between a mother and a son is eternal. The bond between a mother and any of her children is eternal. That bond does not end with the death of either the mother or the child. When my own mother died in 1980, for years afterward, things would happen and I would say to myself, "I have to remember to tell Ma about this." Only then would I remember that she was dead. I'd tell her anyway!

Mothers and sons certainly have their moments, and I am sure that there are days when many Mount mothers would like to send their sons on a rocket to the moon. Those moments, however, pass quickly. How many times in my career have I heard guys tell me that they can hide nothing from their mothers? A mother's intuition is so attuned that she only has to look at her son to know what's going on.

As we celebrate the month of May, all Mount mothers should understand that you are always in your son's mind and in his heart, even on those days when he is not treating you with the love and respect you deserve. If you raised him properly, and I know you have, you have become so much a part of him that he can never escape or deny you. To do that would be to deny himself. Remember that on those days when he is really trying your patience.

May the Mother of God, whom we celebrate in a special way this month, intercede with her Son for the Mount, that all Mount boys might become men of whom their mothers and God can be truly proud.

On Cousin Honey and Mothers

At every junior retreat I give the fourth-day closing talk and, for the last twenty years, even before she died, I have spoken about my Cousin Honey. Her real name is Geraldine Mary Kelly, but for reasons lost in the mists of family history, we always called her Honey. Honey was a registered nurse and an incredibly loving and charitable woman, the unmarried daughter in the Irish family who took care of everybody. Somewhere around 1980, Honey moved to Cape Cod near Provincetown where she was working as a visiting and hospice nurse when the AIDS crisis began. Provincetown had a large gay community and, apparently, no one wanted to nurse these men dying of AIDS. Knowing the woman that Honey was, the visiting nurses asked her to take on these cases, and she did. When she first began to nurse these men, Honey told me that she was not going to become emotionally involved because they were all going to die. Remember, this was during the early days of AIDS. One night I called her, and her father, my uncle, told me that Honey was spending the night with one of "her boys" because he was dying alone. Honey believed that no one should ever die alone. A few days later Honey called me, and she was not happy. "Jimmy, you wouldn't believe it. I called the man's mother and told her who I was, that her son had only forty-eight hours to live, and that she needed to come immediately. She told me she wasn't coming. I thought she hadn't understood me and repeated that her son was dying. She understood. She and her son were estranged because he was gay and dying of AIDS. She wasn't coming."

To say that Honey was appalled is an understatement. Consequently, she began the arduous task of reconciling many of her patients with their estranged families and, in some instances, with God. Honey was an Irish girl with a very persuasive way! Gradually, and not without much emotional pain, she managed to reconcile many of the men and their families. Unfortunately, Honey died of lung cancer at the age of fifty and, at her wake, our family heard countless stories about Honey's care and compassion as a nurse. One woman said to me, "Your cousin made me see sense. Because of her, I was with my son when he died. Imagine the guilt I would have lived with for the rest of my life if I had been stubborn and not been there. Your cousin made me see sense."

There are two points that I make from the Cousin Honey story. The first point is that living the Christian life as she did involves the cross. Honey was willing to pay the emotional price for dealing with the men she nursed and helping them and their families come to peace with one another. Long after these men died, Honey was still dealing with their parents and the residual guilt. As she used to say, "I spend my nights on the phone with the parents of the men I nursed until death." My other collateral point is that the boys on retreat can't possibly imagine that, if they were seriously ill, their mothers wouldn't be rushing to their bedside. I tell them, "You stub your toe or have a fever and your mother is all over you. You can't imagine that if you were seriously ill, she wouldn't be there." By the time I talk, the boys are usually quasi-comatose because they're very tired from the retreat, but I always see recognition in their eyes when I talk about their mothers. They know that I am speaking the truth.

In our nation, May is the month of mothers and, in our Church, it is the month of Mary, the model of all mothers. On Good Friday I attended the Stations of the Cross at the Little Sisters of the Poor. In the meditation for the fourth station, Jesus Meets His Mother, we read, "The disciples fled, yet she did not flee. She stayed there, with a mother's courage, a mother's fidelity, a mother's goodness and a faith which did not waiver in the hour of darkness." Over the years, I have seen those qualities in so many mothers. I watched one mother nurse her son in the last hour of his life under the most trying of circumstances, and she was the one who had the courage to tell the doctors when it was time to let her son go. Over the years, I have witnessed the fact that, in family trials, it is very frequently the mother who has the most courage and who holds everything together. That's one of the reasons why I continually encourage the boys to never do anything that would break their mothers' hearts.

I end my talk describing Honey's very beautiful death. She, who had a principle that no one should die alone, was rewarded by God for her fidelity. She died surrounded by two of her sisters and my sister, women who loved her dearly. The boys chuckle when I tell them about my view of Honey's entrance into heaven. I envision that, at the moment of her death and her arrival at the gates of heaven, the gay men's choir burst into the "Hallelujah Chorus," and all those men and women whom Honey had nursed 'til death carried her to Christ. Of course, Christ and Honey didn't have to be introduced. They knew each other very well. "Whatever you did for the least of my brothers and sisters, you did for me."

Take this month of Mary to thank God for the strength, the courage, and the fidelity of all mothers. You are a gift to your children and a beautiful reflection of the love of God.

SECTION FOUR

THE XAVERIAN BROTHERS

The history and heritage of the Xaverian Brothers are so much a part of who I am that they motivate and inform everything I do, not just in school, but in life. When I was a very young Brother, Brother Aubert Downey taught the novices the history of the Congregation. He always told us that he wanted us to know about "the valiant men who have gone before you and on whose shoulders you stand."

Every year I devote at least one letter to a Xaverian Brother, one who I believe exemplifies the best in our tradition. The boys at Mount Saint Joseph today think, in many ways, that the school dropped out of the sky and really didn't begin to exist until they arrived. I try constantly to dispel that illusion! Our older schools, like Saint X and the Mount, were built on the blood, sweat and tears of generations of Xaverian Brothers. Because of them, we exist today and, thank God, their spirit still informs all that we do. These Brothers are my heritage. These Brothers are the heritage of every school founded by the Xaverian Brothers. They are the Mount's heritage. I hope that is clearly reflected in the letters which follow.

On Brother Paul and 150 Years

On August 2, 2004, the Xaverian Brothers will celebrate the 150th anniversary of our arrival in the United States and the beginning of Xaverian education. When, in 1854, the Brothers began our educational ministry in Louisville, Kentucky, Brother Paul Van Gerwen was the first Superior of the Brothers in the United States. It was Brother Paul, as the Founder of Saint Mary's Industrial School, who brought us to Baltimore in 1868. Brother Paul is one of my heroes and, while he has no direct connection with Mount Saint Joseph, if it were not for Brother Paul's tenacity, the Xaverian Brothers would not have survived in the United States, never mind have founded Mount Saint Joseph. I would like to dedicate this month's letter to Brother Paul.

Born in Gemert, Holland, Brother Paul entered the Xaverian Brothers in May of 1844, five years after the foundation of the Congregation. He was among the first group of Xaverian Brothers who, along with the founder, made their perpetual profession in October of 1847. Theodore Ryken, the founder of the Congregation, chose Brother Paul to lead the first group of Xaverians to Louisville in 1854. After four difficult years, Brother Ryken recalled Brother Paul and all but two of the Xaverians in Louisville to Belgium. Two years later, in 1860, Brother Vincent, the second Superior General, chose Brother

Paul, once again, to lead a second group of Xaverians to Louisville. On the second attempt, the seed took root, and four years later in August of 1864, Brother Paul founded St. Xavier High School. Although the seed took root, the existence of the Xaverian Brothers at that time was rather precarious because of the financial situation at the Mother House. Brother Paul sent every penny he could scrape together back to Belgium to assist the Mother House. During those years, he said to the Brothers that he dreaded opening a letter from Belgium for fear that it would tell him that all was at an end and that the Congregation was suppressed. Because of Brother Paul's efforts to stave off financial disaster at the Mother House, he was called "The Savior of the Congregation." It was also during these years that Brother Paul resisted the efforts of clergy in Kentucky to get him to break with the Mother House and to found an American congregation. He politely, but firmly, refused. Brother Paul had professed his vows as a Xaverian Brother, and a Xaverian Brother he would remain.

In 1868, Brother Paul was called upon to lead the first group of Xaverians in the United States to work outside of the Diocese of Louisville. At the request of Bishop Martin Spalding, Brother Paul and the Xaverians assumed control of St. Mary's Industrial School in Baltimore. Once again, Brother Paul was confronted with very primitive conditions and very difficult circumstances. In 1869, he was recalled to Europe and placed in charge of the struggling Xaverian school in Manchester, England.

In 1872, Brother Paul was once again sent to Louisville to deal with serious difficulties in the Community there. The Community in Louisville had been torn apart because of the Franco-Prussian War. The Superior, Brother Peter Alcantara

Klyberg, was rabidly pro-French in a Community which had a large number of German Brothers. Feeling that they had no voice and no recourse, many of the German Brothers left the Congregation in what the Xaverians refer to as the Schism of 1871. Brother Paul was sent, once again, to Louisville to calm the troubled waters, and it was said that the very mention of his name brought courage to the faint-hearted Brothers in Louisville.

In his biography of Brother Paul, Brother Isidore writes of this same period, "Though the clouds of doubt hovered over the future, he would, under all circumstances, remain faithful to the Congregation to the welfare of which he had dedicated himself." In referring to "the troubles" of 1871 and Brother Paul's reassignment to Louisville in 1872, Brother Julian wrote, "What seemed an inevitable wreck was staved off by the mere presence of this kindly man, who at once established courage in the fainthearted, confidence in the distressed, and strength in all."

Brother Paul spent the last 13 years of his life at St. X, dying there on June 28, 1885. While St. X struggled during Brother Paul's life, after his death, the school began to flourish, and Brothers of his generation attributed the school's success to Brother Paul's heavenly intercession.

Brother Paul's life and the virtues he incarnated in his life can only be understood within the context of his faith. Like the founder of the Xaverian Brothers, Theodore James Ryken, Brother Paul was a man of profound faith, a man who was deeply in love with God and the service of God. Although Brother Paul had been dead for 17 years when St. Xavier in Louisville moved from Fourth Street to Broadway, the Brothers must certainly have had Brother Paul in mind when they inscribed above the altar in the school chapel *Omnia cum Deo, Nihil sine Eo, Everything with God, Nothing without God.* Mount Saint Joseph and each of the other Xaverian schools in the United States stand as a testimony to Brother Paul's faith, and the Mount takes seriously its responsibility to foster in the next generation of Mount men the faith on which Brother Paul founded Xaverian education.

As we begin this 128th school year at the Mount, and as we celebrate 150 years of Xaverian education in the United States, we need to remember Brother Paul. If we do *Everything with God, and Nothing without God*, this school year will be more than a success. It will be a triumph of faith.

On Xaverian Education and Good Role Models

Last week I attended a meeting of the Mount Saint Joseph Hall of Fame committee. As the new kid on the block, I asked a lot of questions. I was particularly interested to see if Saint Joe inducted team managers into the Hall of Fame. Team managers in boys' high school athletics work incredibly hard and don't always get a lot of respect. I know this from personal experience since, thirty-seven years ago, I was the manager for my high school's football and baseball teams. Managing those teams is one of the reasons that I am a teacher today. I attended a co-educational high school run by the Sisters of Saint Joseph of Boston, and while they were superb women and excellent teachers, there weren't many male role models in the school unless you were involved in athletics. Since I wasn't a jock, I was not likely to encounter any coaches. One day, however, the school chaplain, Father Shea, asked if I would consider becoming a manager since there weren't many volunteers. I agreed, not knowing that working as a manager was going to bring me into contact with two men who would become incredibly influential in my life, Paul Cusick, the school's Athletic Director and Joe Guden, a football and basketball coach.

Paul Cusick had a Buick convertible, and, incredibly, he let me drive it—and even trusted me to take the car into Boston to a sports supply store to do his weekly shopping. Today, I would have a serious conversation with any teacher who was silly enough to loan a teenage boy his or her car, but in 1963, Coach Cusick didn't seem to give it a second thought. He was the first adult, apart from my parents, who trusted me. He expected that I would do a good job and that I wouldn't let him down, and because he trusted me, I didn't let him down. He also made me feel like an adult and someone that could handle responsibility and get the job done.

Joe Guden defended me in one of the more embarrassing experiences of my life. We were playing our arch-rival, Matignon, on Thanksgiving Day, and I forgot to bring the practice footballs so that the team could warm up. One coach lit into me, telling me that I had to be the dumbest thing that God ever put on this earth, but Joe Guden came to my defense, telling the other coach that nobody was perfect. He then put his arm around my shoulder and said, "Don't worry about it, Kelly. You made an honest mistake, but now you are going to have to go over to the Matignon coach and ask if we can borrow some footballs. That's going to be embarrassing, but don't grovel. Just put it as a simple question." Joe Guden was probably the first adult who took my side against another adult. When you are sixteen years old, you expect your mother to defend you, but not necessarily a football coach at your school. Paul Cusick and Joe Guden were an integral part of my very positive high school experience, and in thirty years as a teacher, I hope that I have had, in some small way, the positive influence on my students that those two men had on me.

I feel that the essence of Xaverian Brothers' education is relationship. The relationship between the students and the faculty and the relationships among the students are what make Mount Saint Joseph the uniquely Xaverian school that it is. I hope that, in your son's four years at the Mount, he meets a Paul Cusick or a Joe Guden, teachers and coaches who make him feel good about himself and who help him to recognize the talents that he has and the responsibility that he has to develop those talents.

In the original rule of the Xaverian Brothers, dating back to the beginning of the 20th century, it was written:

> The Brothers shall do their best to win the confidence and affection of the pupils, and with this objective in view show interest in them, rejoicing or sympathizing with them like a good father in the midst of his family. They shall closely study the character of each pupil in order to guide him properly.

The language might be paternalistic, but the spirit of that rule is very much alive and well at Mount Saint Joseph. The men and women on the faculty work to win your son's trust and affection so that they can help him grow. I watched that happen during this past summer in summer school, and if it happens during summer school, sometimes under the adverse circumstance of student failure, it most certainly happens every day during the school year. Of course, your son has to do his part. He has to find ways to get involved with the school. Very often a teacher's most profound influence occurs in extracurricular activities, but your son has to be there to reap that benefit. If your son hasn't become involved in the extracurricular life at the school yet, please encourage him to do so during this school year. He may grumble now, but twenty years from now he will be grateful.

Although they were rather young men at the time they came

into my life, Joe Guden and Paul Cusick knew instinctively that it doesn't take much to win the heart of a teenage boy. All you have to do is pay attention to him and let him know that you like him, even on those days when he isn't being very likable. I have often thought what I would have missed if I had said no to Father Shea the day he asked me to be a manager. In many ways, I am the teacher I am today because of those two men.

As we begin this new school year, I pray that your son will find men and women on the faculty of the Mount who will have the same wonderful influence on him, men and women whom he will remember gratefully 30, 40 and 50 years from now. After all, a Mount Saint Joseph education doesn't last for four years. It lasts a lifetime.

On Brother Lambert and a Xaverian Education

On July 15, Mr. Fitzpatrick, Brother Charles, Brother Steve and I took Brother Lambert's niece and nephew out to dinner to celebrate the first anniversary of Brother Lambert's death. Graduating from Mount Saint Joseph in May of 1936, Howard Bents entered the Xaverian Brothers the following November and was given the name Lambert when he received the Holy Habit on Saint Joseph's Day in 1937. A very important man in the Xaverian Brothers, Brother Lambert was the founding Principal of Ryken High School in Leonardtown, Maryland, the Principal of Immaculate Conception Boys' Catholic High School in Malden, Massachusetts, the Director of the CYO Home for Boys in Detroit, Michigan, and the Principal of Holy Name School in Brooklyn, New York. Between his years of being in charge, he taught school, kept the books and managed the plant at a number of schools. Mr. Fitzpatrick had Brother Lambert for U.S. History at Xaverian High School in 1966 and claims that Brother Lambert was one of the finest classroom teachers he had ever had. All of his life, Brother Lambert remained devoted to Mount Saint Joseph where he was stationed twice. From 1949 until 1953, he was the Director of Residents when the Mount was a boarding school, and from 1992 until he retired in 1998, he was the director of our bookstore. You can understand why we thought that a celebration of the anniversary of his entry into heaven was appropriate.

After Brother Lambert died, the Brothers found a letter among his effects which was written to him in 1981 by a man whom he had taught at Mount Saint Joseph in 1953. As I read the letter, I understood clearly why Brother Lambert had kept it for so many years. It is a letter which every teacher hopes to receive at least once in his or her life from a former student. The letter read:

> I owe you quite a bit. I learned a number of things from you in addition to the American History that you pounded into my not terribly willing head. You were the first (and damned near the only) teacher that I had in 20 years of formal education who understood excellence and demanded it of his students. And from you I learned the ideas of perseverance and the joy of mastery. Now I teach about 1,100 students a semester, and the interesting thing is to watch me demanding excellence and forcing students to be concerned with quality. There is very little doubt in my mind as to the impact that you have had on me. As you know better than I, the goal of education is change. From this I can but conclude that you must have been a terribly fine teacher. . . . Indeed, I think one might conclude that if a student can only remember the name of an instructor after a quarter of a century, that instructor must have done something right. In this case I remember considerably more and can even quote you on academic performance, particularly on my academic performance when my usual A grade slipped to C+ one time because of indolence. You saw to it that the situation did not recur.

This letter not only says a great deal about Brother Lambert, it also articulates very clearly the Xaverian Brothers' philosophy of education. What Brother Lambert did for his former student at the Mount in 1953, the faculty at Mount Saint Joseph strives to do every day with your sons. Are we always successful? Perhaps not. But I think that we have far more hits than misses. Of course, the problem is that teenage boys, if they recognize what is being done for them, are rarely able to express any gratitude. That comes later, even 30 years later, when they have had time to mature and to reflect on what was done for them. Recently, Mr. Lilley shared with me a similar letter which he had received from a man who graduated from the Mount 20 years ago. A few weeks ago, I also heard from a man whom I had taught in 1984, telling me that he was about to make his final vows as a Jesuit and thanking me for being a positive influence in his life. I told Mr. Fitz that letter would keep me going for at least five more years!

Academic excellence and enduring personal relationships are the cornerstones of Xaverian education. Every day, as I wander the corridors of the Mount, I see these elements of Xaverian education at work in the faculty of the Mount. I don't expect your son to come to Mount Saint Joseph everyday overwhelmed with gratitude for what his teachers are trying to do for him. That would be expecting far too much from the teenage psyche. Twenty years from now, however, I trust that your son will look back at Mount Saint Joseph with gratitude and, even if he doesn't write a letter of gratitude to one of his former teachers, I am sure that the names of at least a few of his teachers will occasionally run through his mind and bring a grateful smile to his face.

As we begin this new school year, please pray with me that the Mount faculty will meet the challenges of educating in the Xaverian tradition, and please pray with me that, during this school year, your son will find his Brother Lambert on the Mount Saint Joseph faculty.

On Brother Eric, Brother Carlos and Xaverian Education

Henry A. Magruder and Carl A. Magruder, blood brothers from Louisville, Kentucky, both entered the Xaverian Brothers on January 6, 1933. As Brother Eric and Brother Carlos, these two men together gave Mount Saint Joseph fifty-nine years of service. While Brother Eric died at the early age of forty-five, Brother Carlos lived to be eighty-nine. During World War II, when the army needed draftsmen, Brother Carlos and Brother Eric were trained to teach mechanical drawing at Mount Saint Joseph and were stationed here together, something that rarely happened with blood brothers in the Xaverian Brothers in those days.

Brother Eric was missioned at Mount Saint Joseph for sixteen years, directing the Industrial Arts department and having a profound impact on the young men whom he taught. At a recent alumni gathering, a graduate of the Class of 1949 told me that he owed everything that he has become professionally to Brother Eric. All of the alumni who knew him speak of him with love and affection. Brother Eric was transferred to Saint Xavier in Louisville at the end of the 1956-1957 school year, but as soon as he arrived at Saint X, he became seriously ill with Hodgkin's Disease. He was sent back to the Mount to die. His obituary reads, "Brother Eric was returned to the Mount, his great love, the school which had been his field of action for years."

Shortly before he died, Brother Eric wrote to Brother Thomas More, the Principal at Saint X, "Thanks for having the medical report sent to me. As you and I know, it is not good. I have been confined to bed since Monday. I have lost control of my lower limbs, but I hope that they will come back. I am resigned to God's will. Twenty-five years ago I offered my life to Him, and now it is in His hands." Brother Thomas More once told me the story of Brother Eric's final days at Saint X. He was seriously ill and could no longer teach. One day a group of boys came to Brother Thomas More and told him that Brother Eric was back in his classroom. Brother Thomas More found Brother Eric in the mechanical drawing room, holding himself up on the teacher's desk. He said, "I had to give it one last try." Brother Thomas More helped him back to his room in the Brother's house and, shortly after that, he was returned to the Mount. That "one last try" spoke eloquently, not only of his will-power, but of his dedication to his vocation. He died on his brother's birthday, March 1, 1958.

Brother Carlos spent seven years at the Mount with his brother during the 1940s and returned in 1970 for a twenty-six-year assignment as Director of the Plant, Superior of the Brothers' community and moderator of the Mothers' Club. Since Brother Carlos did not teach during his last, long assignment to the Mount, he is perhaps best remembered by the faculty, the staff and the Mothers' Club. His dedication to the Mount was unstinting, taking meticulous care of all of the little details which make a large and rambling school plant run smoothly. He was a man who had an infinite capacity for minding the details. Confined to a nursing home in his final years, he died in 2003 after much suffering. In his eulogy, it was written, "Loyalty was woven through the sinews of his body and ran through the deepest part of him. His two great loyalties were Mount Saint Joseph and the Xaverian Congregation. The Mount, his first and last mission, became a place deeply engraved in his heart—a place fraught with so many memories that the recollection of them often brought tears to his eyes." I visited Brother Carlos in the last days of his life as his mind was failing. We sat in his room at the Nazareth Nursing Home under a picture of the Mount tower. At first, he didn't remember who I was and, even as he remembered my name, I doubt that he knew at that point that I was the President of the Mount. As our conversation progressed, I realized that, in Carlos' mind, we were not at the Nazareth Nursing Home, so I asked him, "Carlos, where are we?" He replied, "Why, we're at the Mount of course." Truly Mount Saint Joseph was engraved in his heart.

Mr. Fitz speaks to the boys at the Mount about "standing on the shoulders of Giants." Brother Eric and Brother Carlos are two of those Giants who incarnated in their lives the virtues of zeal, simplicity, trust, humility, and compassion which are the foundation stones of Xaverian education, virtues which we attempt to inculcate in every Mount student. My job as the President of the school and Mr. Fitzpatrick's job as Principal is to make sure that, from their place in heaven, Brother Eric and Brother Carlos are smiling down on the Mount, still recognizing in it the very Xaverian and very Catholic school to which they gave their lives. As we begin this school year, I pray that the Mount will become for your son the very special place that it was to Brother Eric and Brother Carlos and that your son may grow in those virtues which are the hallmark of Xaverian education.

On the Continuing Legacy of the Mount

> I visited two classes. In each I saw good strong work, though I thought it was somewhat formal. The surroundings were in every way favorable to good teaching. The Brothers have plenty of subject matter, and they certainly have a keen understanding of boy nature. Owing, I suspect, to the strong science work in this school, I believe that the teaching as a whole is more closely connected with current life than in any other of the parochial schools I have visited. . . . I recommend that Mount Saint Joseph College High School be placed upon our approved list of private High Schools for 1922–1923.
>
> Report to Superintendent Albert S. Cook on examination of Mount Saint Joseph College, Irvington, Maryland, April 18, 1923 by Samuel M. North, Supervisor High Schools

We lost a good deal of the Mount's archives when Alexius Hall was razed in 1981. I introduced you to Brother Carlos Magruder in the last letter, but while Brother Carlos was a very holy man and a super teacher, he had no sense of history and consigned over 100 years worth of history to the dumpster. Today, we can't find the original college records dating back to the days when Mount Saint Joseph was a degree-granting institution. Since the Mount was the Xaverian Brothers' Mother House from 1876 until the early 1970s, much Xaverian history was lost as well. Schools have a tendency to accumulate junk, and we have old computers, spare parts for computers, old desks, trophies that cannot be identified and heaven knows what else tucked into every corner of this institution. There are days when I would like to bring Brother Carlos back from eternity just for a week or two to clean out the place. Before he came, however, I would go through the junk to make sure that he threw out nothing of historical value.

The paragraph which forms the epigraph of this letter is from a 1923 report from the State of Maryland accrediting the Mount as a private school. I don't know how it escaped Brother Carlos, but it did. This report was prepared during the last year that Brother James Garrity was the Headmaster at Mount Saint Joseph. He died in office as did his successor, Brother Antoninus. The redoubtable Brother James was an exacting school master, tolerating no nonsense and brooking no opposition. He had been the Headmaster of Saint Xavier in Louisville for thirty-two years before he came to the Mount in 1917. Brother James was a man who applied rigorous academic standards to the schools over which he presided. During his days in Louisville, any boy who made three incorrect responses during any recitations in the school day had to stay after school until he knew the subject matter sufficiently to please Brother James. Brother James also had the habit of reading the grades for the entire school out loud at a public assembly. Pity the boy whose grades were below par. Of course, in those long ago days, the Mount had only 144 students in the high school, 108 of whom were boarders. There was also a grammar school. The faculty consisted of eight Xaverian Brothers. Both Mr. Fitz and I would think we had died and gone to heaven if we only had to deal with 144 boys and we had eight Brothers to teach them. Mr. Fitz could play golf most days and not worry about the school, and I could relax and not worry about money since the Brothers took no salary.

The most telling thing in the report, to my mind, is the observation that the Brothers have "a keen understanding of boy nature." That is one of the Mount's great strengths, and it is as true today as it was in 1923. Boys are our specialty. There is very little about the teenage boy that we don't know and haven't seen thousands of times before. Mr. Fitz and I have 80 years of combined experience working with teenage boys and, since our faculty has a strong number of veterans like Mr. Rukowicz, Mr. Cegelski and Mr. McDivitt who have been at the Mount for over forty years, as well as many others who have been here over twenty-five years, we do know "boy nature" inside out and backwards.

The report of 1923 goes on to state, "Owing, I suspect, to the strong science work in the school, I believe that the teaching as a whole is more closely connected with current life than in any other of the parochial schools I have visited." Well, we certainly are still a strong science school. Whether that relates us to current life or not, I don't know. I do know that training the boys to become productive and caring men in this modern world is the focus of all of our effort. Brother James Garrity prided himself on the good, Catholic men whom Saint Xavier High School in Louisville and the Mount produced during his tenure as Headmaster in both schools. Having followed Brother's example as Headmaster of both Saint X and the Mount, I have a similar pride. Mount Saint Joseph takes boys and, together with their parents and guardians, we work to turn those boys into men, men who matter, Mount men.

Knowing that Brother James Garrity, Brother Carlos and all of the Brothers and lay people associated with the Mount who are now with God are praying with us for the success of this school year, let's begin the 131st year in the Mount's history.

On Brother Declan and Ashes to Easter

On February 9, 2006, Brother Declan Kane went home to God after a long struggle with cancer. Entering the Xaverian Brothers in 1951, Brother Declan spent thirty-six of his fifty-four years as a Xaverian Brother at Mount Saint Joseph. For at least two generations of Mount men, Brother Declan *was* the Mount, a living symbol of the school. Given his long association with the Mount, we wanted to give him a splendid send-off, and that we did. His wake was held in the auditorium where a steady stream of his former students and friends came to pay their respects. He was buried from Saint Mark's Church in Catonsville where the 250 boys in the Mount's senior class served as honor guard for his obsequies. Brother Declan would have appreciated the tribute. He always loved Christmas, and his funeral liturgy began with "O Come All Ye Faithful." The heavy snowfall the day before his wake, which didn't seem to dampen the attendance, would have also delighted his heart. No doubt he was smiling in heaven!

As Lent begins, Brother Declan's wake and funeral put me in one of my reflective moods. Most Xaverian Brothers die much more anonymous deaths than Brother Declan. He had the privilege of being stationed at one school for almost all of his adult life, and he remained in Baltimore after his retirement, staying in touch with the Mount and his many former students. Most Brothers end their lives in one of our retirement homes and often have no real association with the schools on whose campuses they reside. During my years at Saint Xavier in Louisville, our retirement home, Ryken House, filled and emptied twice as the retired Brothers died. Their funerals were held in the school chapel with only the local Brothers and my English class in attendance. From the Saint X chapel, pallbearers, chosen from my English class, would carry the Brother to the cemetery which is also on the grounds of the school. I always told the kids stories about the Brother whose funeral they were attending and whose remains they were carrying to the grave, so that they would have some sense of the life of dedicated religious service which the Brother had lived. Rarely were any of the Brother's former students present for his funeral, and since many of our Brothers live to a very ripe old age, they are often buried without any family present other than their Xaverian family.

There is an old Catholic adage that there is nothing deader than a dead monk. When we die, there are no progeny to carry on the name, no children at the bedside, no wife to grieve. It sounds rather sad, doesn't it? Fortunately, it's not because of our hope in Christ. I remember the funeral of Brother Francis which I attended as an eighteen-year-old novice in 1965. Brother had died of a brain tumor, and the undertaker hadn't even bothered to take the bandages off his head for his wake. Dressed in his habit and laid out in a plain wooden box, he looked very dead, the deadest person I had ever seen. No flowers adorned the coffin which was flanked only by the Paschal candle. I don't remember if my novice master, Brother Kevin, did any catechesis with us after Brother Francis's funeral, but if he did, I suspect he told us that our belief in the Resurrection is so strong that we don't need any trappings to make death look like anything other than it is, the end of one life and the beginning of a new one. Brother Declan went home to God with a multitude of former students coming to pay their respects, a symbol of all of the lives Brother Declan had touched in his life. Yet the Brothers who die much more anonymous deaths also bring with them to God all of the boys whom they have taught, all of the colleagues with whom they have ministered and all of the good works of a life well-lived.

When I entered the Xaverian Brothers in 1965, we ended the day with the following prayer:

> Jesus, Mary and Joseph, I give you my heart and my soul. Jesus, Mary and Joseph, grant me the grace of final perseverance (in my vocation as a Brother). Jesus, Mary and Joseph, may I breathe forth my soul in peace with you.

I don't know if Brother Declan often said this prayer after we ceased to say it as a community, but with God's grace, those petitions certainly came true in his life. Over the last forty years, I have lived with and known more Brothers than I could count who have gone home to God and, like Brother Declan, they have all died quite peacefully. Perhaps that is because they know that they have everything to hope for. Lent reminds all of us that, with Christ, we live through the ashes of life in the sure hope of sharing in His Resurrection. That's an awesome hope!

On Brother Dominic and One Hundred and Thirty Years

During this month, Mount Saint Joseph celebrates the 130th anniversary of its founding. Brother Alexius, the provincial superior of the Brothers in the United States from 1875 until 1903, appointed Brother Dominic O'Connell, a native of Ireland, as the first principal of Mount Saint Joseph. As you will see, the relationship between Brother Dominic and Brother Alexius was a rather complicated one, but the choice of Brother Dominic to begin Mount Saint Joseph certainly showed a great deal of wisdom on Brother Alexius' part. Brother Dominic was a man of great heart, compassionate and loving to all whom he encountered. When he died in 1907, the *Baltimore American* wrote, "No box was in the grave to keep out the earthdamp and the elements, which bring about the return of the flesh to the earth whence it came, and no stone will tell the passer-by that he is walking by what remains of the earthly temple of one of the most unselfish and most Christian characters that Baltimore has ever known... Hundreds turned out to pay their last tribute to the man of God, who had for a generation worked among the people of Baltimore, helping wayward boys to turn about in their paths of recklessness and lead better lives." This is the man who set the earliest foundations for Mount Saint Joseph.

Brother Dominic left the Mount in 1883 and became the principal and superior of Saint Patrick's School in Lowell, Massachusetts, where he led a group of Brothers who taught some rather tough Irish immigrant boys during the day and their fathers at night. Realizing how overworked his community of Brothers was, Brother Dominic arranged for them to have a week's outing at a lake in New Hampshire. During that outing, there was a boating accident, and, unfortunately, only one of the Brothers in the boat, young Brother Bonaventure, was able to swim. Securing his confreres to the overturned boat, Brother Bonaventure swam towards the shore, but exhausted from helping his Brothers, he drowned. The provincial, Brother Alexius, held Brother Dominic responsible for Brother Bonaventure's death since Brother Dominic had not sought permission for this outing. It was an era without telephones, and the mail was slow. Brother Dominic did what his great heart told him needed to be done and gave his overworked community a refreshing break. Brother Alexius removed Brother Dominic as principal and superior of Saint Patrick's and sent him to Saint Mary's Industrial School to teach the grammar grades. Obedient and humble, Brother Dominic repaired to Saint Mary's without a grumble or complaint and began his new work. He was too great a man to let his public humiliation in being removed from office deter his work for his boys. During his time at Saint Mary's, he came to the attention of Cardinal Gibbons, who immediately told Brother Alexius that Brother Dominic should be in charge of Saint Mary's. Brother Alexius, of course, had to bow to the Cardinal! With his appointment as the superior at Saint Mary's, Brother Dominic was able to begin his great life's work defending poor, homeless and delinquent boys. His love for the poor was so great that he founded a number of protective institutions for homeless boys which the Xaverian Brothers staffed through the first half of the twentieth century, closing the last one, Don Bosco Hall in Detroit, in 1965. The late Brother Lambert, who was a Mount alumnus and who spent many years here on the faculty, was the last superior in Detroit.

With the death of Brother Alexius in 1900, Brother Dominic was elected provincial by the Brothers, who always knew that it was his great heart which had caused him the trouble with Brother Alexius. The Brothers loved Brother Dominic as he loved them. As Brother Julian wrote in his history of the Xaverian Brothers, *Men in Deeds*, “Good Brother Dominic! As Provincial he was loved. None could possibly associate fear with him.” When Brother Dominic died in 1907, basically from overwork, not only was his community of Xaverian Brothers heart-broken, but all of Baltimore grieved with them as well.

In his life and in his words, Brother Dominic had one message for his Brothers, all of whom were either teaching boys in our schools or caring for them in our protective institutions. The message was always: “Take good care of the boys.” He had made it his life’s work to take good care of the boys, and that is the legacy, along with his great heart, which he has left to Mount Saint Joseph. Every day at the Mount, the members of our faculty take good care of the boys, and the boys take good care of one another. Oh, of course, we have occasional altercations between students and occasional disagreements among the faculty, but the overriding tone of the school reflects Brother Dominic’s great heart and his admonition to take good care of the boys.

The Mount is a school of great heart, and I know that, every day, Brother Dominic looks down from his place in heaven with great pride in this school which he began so humbly in 1876. Let's pray together that the Mount will always be worthy of Brother Dominic's legacy.

On Brothers Hilary and Rudolph and the Unchanging Nature of the Teenage Male

During this past summer, I discovered two essays, written by Brothers long dead, reflecting on their first year as a teacher in the late 1930s. As I read these essays, I was struck by the unchanging nature of the adolescent male. Reflections by Brothers on their work in education 50 and 60 years ago are as relevant today as they were when they were written.

Commenting on his first day in the classroom at Saint X in Louisville in 1939, the late Brother Hilary Murphy wrote in 1944:

> They were studying me, those most clairvoyant of critics, and I knew I would be cataloged and indexed long before I could do the same with them. Be natural, prudence advised me; they can spot any affectation and will act the same way toward you. They were interested in me as a new teacher, and I was certainly interested in them. The admonition of my wise old novice master crept into my mind. Be business-like; get right down to work; don't waste any time building up a case for yourself, but let your actions do it. Set the tone of your class, and the boys will take up the same key. Be neither too tyrannical, nor too easy-going, just be industrious.

As I read those words of Brother Hilary, I was reminded of my own mentor during my early years, the late Brother Ivan Corkery, who was my first Superior. He used to tell the young Brothers in his community, "Have ninety minutes of work prepared for every forty-five minute class. Keep them so busy that they have no time to give you any trouble." Brother Ivan would tell us that the boys would respect us if, and only if, we taught them well. You can work them to death and be rigorous in discipline provided that they feel that they are learning. Of course, they never let you know how they feel! More often than not, they complain about the work and the discipline. If you are lucky, you will find out about the respect and the gratitude years later.

As I have told you many times in the past, teaching and parenting run on the same track. The busier you keep your son, the less trouble you are going to have with him. If he is involved with extra-curricular activities at school, such as sports or clubs, or with the Boy Scouts or with his church youth group, he won't have too much time to give you trouble. Between his extra-curricular involvements and his school work, he should be more than busy. The old adage, "The idle mind is the devil's workshop," is particularly true with teenage boys.

After a fifty-year career in the classroom, Brother Rudolph reflected on his first year teaching, also at Saint X, in the late 1930s:

> I learned—but ever so slowly—that way down in just about every American kid's heart there's an innate decency and friendliness that generally surface if the teacher can wait long enough. That Tom or Joe or Henry or whatever his name is has a surprisingly keen aesthetic sense and will more than

> likely bewilder you with an intuitive grasp of what is good and true and beautiful in literature in general and in poetry in particular. That the American youngster of high school age has an absolute hatred of injustice, particularly when it comes from a teacher, that the student has admiration—concealed, of course, because of peer pressure—for the teacher who's master of the subject that he is teaching and conducts a class without too much buffoonery permitted.

How true that is! Brother Ivan used to tell us, as well, that we always had to be fair with the boys, that injustice from a teacher was intolerable. I think that Brother Ivan would have defined fair as consistent. You have to teach them according to consistent rules where there are consistent consequences. Again, you can work them to death as long as they know what the rules are and that you intend to abide by them and that you are going to treat every boy the same. Nothing undermines a teacher's credibility with his class more quickly than the teacher who has pets. The kids will understand your liking some kids better than others because they like some kids better than others; however, treatment from a teacher has to be the same for all. Of course, there are exceptions when the teacher knows things that the other students in his class don't know about a particular boy's situation. In those cases, I think compassion on the teacher's part has to trump the perceptions of his class. I bet you have had circumstances like that with your own son where he might claim that you are more understanding with one of his siblings than you are with him. As parents, you know that perhaps one of your children more often needs a pat on the back while another one of your children more often need a good swift kick. That is the tightrope you walk as parents and that we walk as teachers. But fairness certainly has to be the bottom line. Having taught English literature for over thirty years, I can attest to Brother Rudolph's insight about boys and poetry. There are times where they just knock my socks off with their intuitive appreciation of what is beautiful in literature.

I think Brother Rudolph's conclusion is very appropriate. Substitute parenting for teaching, and I'm sure you will agree:

> Rewarding? Teaching certainly is. Frustrating? Again, and again, and again! Funny? Sometimes a veritable comedy of errors! Interesting? It is the most fascinating profession in the world. Important? All of those kids who sit before you in the classroom are tomorrow's adults who'll fashion a cosmos that you will love or a universe that you will despise.

Your sons are the future of our country and of the world. You and I, as teachers and parents, had better be doing a good job, so that they will see to it that the future is something of which we can be proud.

On Brother Terence and Humility

Years ago, Brother Thomas Ryan and I interviewed Sister Julie Kildery about her brother, Brother Terence Kildery, who died as a Xaverian Brother at the young age of twenty-five in 1934. Sister Julie must have been in her nineties at the time, and Brother Thomas and I were doing some "oral history" on our deceased Brothers. Brother Terence's obituary was written by his former teacher, Brother Aubert Downey, and, in the obituary, Brother Aubert wrote that even as he was dying, Brother Terence was still, "the tall, handsome young man who exuded charm and fraternal charity." Sister Julie told us that Terence's mother had grave misgivings about the fact that he was so handsome. "Too good looking for his own good, and no good will come of it" she opined. His mother got that one wrong. He died at a young age, a very holy death as a good religious. Apparently, Mrs. Kildery was not overly concerned about boosting her son's ego and enhancing his self-esteem.

Last spring, Brother Daniel Skala, Headmaster of Xaverian Brothers' High School in Westwood, Massachusetts, wrote to the parents of his school about some of the problems we experience with teenage boys and narcissism. We are so concerned today about boosting their self-esteem that we can quite unwittingly create monsters who somehow think they are privileged beyond words and above the law. In our enthusiasm to make them feel good about themselves, we forget to inculcate in them the very important Christian virtue of humility. When I see a sense of humility in a boy, I always attribute it to a good upbringing. And I do see it in some of the smartest and most talented of young men. Unfortunately, however, it is becoming an increasingly rare quality.

I remember one young man in my career who was a very talented athlete and rather cocky about it. Being ever the teacher, I was constantly harassing him about recognizing that his abilities were a gift from his parents' gene pool and, ultimately, from God, and that he needed to exercise those talents with humility. He always looked at me as if I were a tad crazy. But I am right on that. We have to find ways to inculcate in our sons and students a sense of humility, a realization that all of life is a gift, a gift for which we are responsible. Trying to build up their egos without developing in them a sense of humility is a recipe for disaster. We will have a generation of young people who feel entitled simply because we have repeatedly told them how talented they are.

As I mentioned above, I have seen profound humility in some of the most talented boys I have taught over the years. I have also seen profound depression in the most talented boys. I think these are two sides of the same coin. A young man, recognizing his talents and abilities, can become depressed at the very thought of the responsibility of dealing with it all and of the expectations put on him by people who might simply be trying to boost his ego. Finding the right balance here is a tricky business.

There is a rather sad ending to the story of Brother Terence and Sister Julie, which has nothing to do with the topic of this letter, but which I find interesting. Brother Terence was dying at the Massachusetts General Hospital, and his sister was stationed at a convent only ten minutes away. Our Provincial Superior begged her Superior to let her visit her brother. "He is dying a terribly painful death of cancer at such a young age, and it would mean so much to him to see his sister once before he died." The Mother Superior explained that she could not allow Sister Julie to visit her brother because it was against the rules of their order. Imagine a religious order having a rule so blatantly contrary to the dictates of Christian charity. Fortunately, we religious orders have gotten a bit more charitable in the last seventy years.

Do whatever you can to build your son's ego so that he has a truly humble appreciation for his gifts and talents. Help him to recognize and understand that all he has are, indeed, gifts from God, gifts for which he can offer thanks by developing them to the best of his ability. All of this is a tricky business, but being parents is a tricky business as you so well know. I will pray for your success!

On Brother Kevin and Motivation

Recently, I visited my good friend, Brother Giles, at Ryken House, our retirement home in Louisville, Kentucky. At the age of eighty-one, Brother Giles has been a Xaverian Brother for sixty-three years. Although he is nineteen years older than I and nineteen years longer in religious life, we both had the same novice master for our training, Brother Kevin Kenney. Brother Kevin was the novice master for the Xaverian Brothers from 1942 until 1967. Brother Giles was in one of his first classes of novices, and I was in his next-to-last class. On the day of his death, Brother Kevin had formed over fifty percent of the living community of American Brothers and many more of the Brothers who were already with God. And probably each one of those Brothers will give you a different opinion of Brother Kevin. I loved him. Brother Giles was less enthusiastic! His methods were not always enlightened, but he did know that he couldn't treat us all the same, that we were all unique in our own way and required individual attention.

Brother Giles and I were apparently quite different, as witness encounters we each had with Brother Kevin about whether we should continue in our vocation as Xaverian Brothers. One day, Brother Kevin approached Brother Giles and said rather abruptly, "Why don't you go home?" To this Brother Giles replied, "I will not." Now, you have to understand that

Brother Kevin could send anyone home at the drop of a hat. In fact, he did. If Brother Kevin wanted Brother Giles gone, gone he would be. Apparently he was only trying to stiffen Brother Giles' resolve and, given the fact that Brother Giles is still with us more than sixty years later, Brother Kevin's tactic apparently worked. I, on the other hand, presented myself to Brother Kevin and told him that I wanted to go home. He quoted Canon Law to me. He said, "I'm the novice master. I decide who has a vocation and who doesn't. You do. Now go to the chapel, thank God for your vocation and go back to work." Rather befuddled, I did what he told me, and forty-four years later, I'm still here.

One of the more difficult lessons every teacher, as well as every parent, has to learn is what motivates an individual student. In the days when we had forty or more students in a classroom, that wasn't always an easy lesson to learn. Survival was the order of the day when you were teaching over two hundred boys each school day. Relatively early on in my career, I remember realizing that some boys needed the pat on the back while others needed the kick in the butt. Sometimes you kicked the one who needed the pat and patted the one who needed the kick. You learned fairly quickly of your error. Given the fact that kids today live in an electronic society which constantly entertains them, motivating them for solid academic work is even trickier. Education is not about entertainment. It is about stretching the mind, testing its limits, and learning to think critically. I always thought that it was Shakespeare who wrote "Knowledge maketh a bloody entrance," but Google tells me I'm wrong. Regardless of who penned that phrase, they must once have tried to teach adolescents!

Of course, as parents, you have a far more focused audience, but you still have to learn what works and what doesn't. What is the key to motivating your son, and how can you best use that key to set him on the road to maturity? That's not a rhetorical question!

Brother Kevin was a firm believer that his novices had to learn to fly on their own. Once you made your first vows, he kicked you quite firmly out of the nest and sent you on your way. He had done his job, and he expected you to do yours. About twenty years after I left the novitiate, I was at a late-night meeting of the board of Malden Catholic where Brother Kevin was stationed. I had to drive back to Connecticut where I was principal, and I stopped in the Brothers' community room to grab a soda to keep me awake on my way. Brother Kevin came into the community room, looked at me and said, "You look so tired. Come and give your old novice master a hug." I laughed and remarked that if he had seen me hugging another brother when I was a novice, he would have thrown me out. He laughed as well and replied, "I've had a new insight in my old age!" He then told me that he was proud of me, that I was doing good work for the Congregation, and that I needed to take care of myself because the Congregation needed me. He still had the touch with motivation! I drove home far less tired than I was before I encountered him.

Motivation. It's the key to life's success. You and I need to find that key. What works with one boy won't work with another. Find whatever works and use it to set him on the path to maturity.

SECTION FIVE

Advent and Christmas

"Batting out" monthly newsletters for twenty-six years can, at times, be daunting, but I am never daunted when it comes to the liturgical seasons of Advent and Christmas. These are my two favorite seasons in the Church's year of grace.

The longing of the Church for the coming of Christ at Christmas is beautifully echoed in the prophet Isaiah, and the joy of the angels on Christmas day is the joy of the Church as it stands in wonder and awe at the mystery of the Incarnation, the birth of Emmanuel, God-with-us. Writing about that beautiful mystery is never daunting.

I hope the following letters will help us all prepare for the wonder of the Incarnation and the birth of the Lord.

I particularly need to thank Mrs. Triplett of Louisville, whose son Travis I taught at St. X. She had kept all of my letters and was able to supply me with the Christmas letters I had lost.

On Advent

The Church has just begun the beautiful season of Advent, the time of preparations for Christmas when the Church longs for the birth of the Messiah. All of the readings during Advent express the Church's longing for the coming of Christ in the hearts of the faithful at Christmas. Many people, even devout Catholics, do not realize that Advent is a penitential season, a "little Lent." During Advent, as during Lent, we do not say the Gloria at Mass. Those of you who were alive before Vatican II will remember that there were even days of fasting during Advent.

I have always thought that Advent is the perfect season for parents because it is about waiting and, if you think about it, you have spent much of your son's life waiting. You have probably spent hours in a car waiting for his practices or activities to be over, but, more than that, you have waited to see signs of maturity and signs that he is becoming the man you hope he will be. At times during his teenage years, that waiting can take on a rather urgent note. There are certainly days when you ask yourself, somewhat desperately, "Will he ever grow up?" That may be a day when you have had to pick up after him or remind him a hundred times about things that he is supposed to do. Those are the days when he just doesn't seem to show any signs of becoming responsible for himself and for his life. Advent is a time when the Church waits patiently for the coming of the Messiah. During your son's adolescence, your waiting may become rather impatient.

Watching teenage boys grow up is one of the joys and frustrations of being a school teacher. We see definite signs during high school, but we do not get to see the end result. Last month, and for the first time in thirty years, I had the joy of meeting a boy whom I had taught in 1971, my first year teaching. Of course, he is no longer a boy. He is a forty-seven-year-old man, and he is bald! When he was a student, I saw definite signs that things were going to turn out very well for him, and those signs were correct.

Every day at the Mount, I watch the boys whom I taught and the boys whom I got to know last year, growing and taking on new responsibilities, showing definite signs of becoming the Mount men we hope that they will be. Of course, I do not have to live with them as you do, and I do not have as vested an interest in their maturing as you do, but let me assure you that your son will grow up and that your patient waiting will bear fruit. I have seen it happen so many times over the last thirty years that I have incredible confidence in the power of God's grace to turn boys into men.

God's grace does, however, need parental support to work His wonders. The pushing and the prodding that you do, the holding him responsible for his actions, and the ceaseless prayer you offer for his well-being are all the means of God's grace in his young life.

When I was a student at Marian High School, my father kicked me in the butt when I failed Religion and Latin. He conspired with my teacher for both subjects, Sister Anna Catherine, and together they became an unbeatable team against which I was unable to defend myself. My dad and

Sister Anna Catherine became the means of God's grace for me at that time of my life, although I am sure, at the time, my parents were probably wondering if I would ever grow up. I went on to earn a Bachelor's degree in Latin and Greek, and I became a religious. I have always thought that was one of God's little jokes.

As we celebrate Advent with the Church, be patient. With God's grace and your prodding, your son will grow up and become the man God wants him to be. It is just going to take a little patience on your part. Let Advent remind you of that.

On Preparing the Way of the Lord

> The voice of one crying in the desert,
> "Prepare the way of the Lord,
> make straight his paths."
>
> Isaiah 40: 3

The beautiful season of Advent is my favorite season of the Liturgical year. The readings at Mass and the Divine Office from the prophet Isaiah express eloquently our longing for the coming of the Messiah, while John the Baptist, Christ's Herald, reminds us to "Prepare the way of the Lord." Christ is coming, and we need to make straight the paths before Him.

Parents and teachers in a Catholic high school have one job in common, and that job is to prepare the way of the Lord in the hearts of our sons and students. Education in faith begins in the home and is augmented by the Catholic school. Once the seeds of faith have been sown in a young man's heart by his parents, then the Catholic school can provide some of the fertilizer to help those seeds grow. There have been hundreds of books written on theories of adolescent faith development, but I look at it rather simply. Growth of faith in an adolescent is always slow, much slower than parents and teachers would probably like. I've often seen faith only flower in former students of mine when they are married and have their first child. Then they realize that they can't raise that child without God, and faith, once again, becomes important for them.

The novelist and *Newsweek* columnist, Anna Quindlen, is rather liberal politically and, apparently, one of her critics once accused her of not being devoutly Catholic. She replied that the person making that judgment obviously had not been in her house on Sunday mornings when she was forcing her children to attend Mass much to their displeasure. I suspect you have been in that position many times. Faith cannot be forced, but parents can make their position clear by requiring children to attend church as long as the children are living in their house and dependent upon their support. The nature of adolescent faith development is not going to change, but I do think that parents can "prepare the way of the Lord" by making it clear where they stand on matters of faith. Of course, it all comes back to example. If Mom and Dad are attending Mass or church services regularly, junior is going to understand this is an important value to his parents. He may not be ready to accept it now, but when he has his own children, he probably will realize what I said above, that raising children is a formidable task and that raising them without God makes the task even more formidable.

The Mount Saint Joseph alma mater begins, "Hail, Mount Saint Joseph High, Hail, alma mater. Hail, Guardian of our Youth." The Mount's job is to guard your son's youth and to set him on straight paths, preparing the way for the Lord. That is also a formidable task, and we can only accomplish it if the school and his parents are working together for the same end. May the good Lord help all of us, teachers and parents, to prepare God's way in the heart of your son.

Drop down dew, you heavens from above, and let the clouds rain the just One.

On Advent and Not Missing the Moment

Let the earth be opened and bud forth a Savior.

From the Divine Office for Advent

When I entered the novitiate of the Xaverian Brothers in 1965, it was high on a hill above the Charles River in Newton Highlands, Massachusetts. The novitiate was a castle-like structure with a huge clock tower and, because of its position on the hill, it was a very cold place in the winter. Despite the winter cold, I have some very warm memories of my two years there, and one of the warmest is of the time I spent sitting in the chapel on a cold winter's evening reading Pius Parsch's *The Church's Year of Grace*. It was during those winter evenings, as I listened to the wind and the snow howling outside, that I first fell in love with the Church's Advent season. The beautiful readings from Isaiah and the beautiful responses of the Divine Office articulate so very clearly the longing of the Church for the coming of Christ at Christmas and the longing of the Jews for the coming of the Messiah over the long centuries of the Old Testament. Advent is about waiting and patience. Perhaps that is why the season means so much to me, as I am not a very patient man! Advent reminds me that God functions on His own time schedule and not on mine.

We spend so much of our life waiting. In lines at the supermarket, in doctors' offices, in traffic on the beltway, we wait. You're waiting this very moment for your son to grow up. The problem with waiting is that we frequently miss the moment as we anticipate the end of our waiting. Advent always reminds me that the waiting is important in itself and that the moments of waiting are precious. The day will come when your son is grown and gone, and I suspect at that time you will have occasions when you long for the boy that he was and wonder if you missed some of those precious moments.

I have a picture in my office of my godson, his wife and their three daughters. Colin and his family are very precious to me. The other day I found a picture of Colin and me when Colin was twelve, and that picture brought back a flood of memories of the boy he was. He is thirty-four years old now, and I wonder where the last twenty-two years went, wishing that I had even more memories of his boyhood.

Mr. Fitz frequently tells the seniors that, when they are walking up the Cathedral sanctuary to receive their diploma, they will have no more time to make Mount Saint Joseph memories. He wants them to enjoy each moment of their days at the Mount and to make those memories. Let Advent remind you that, as you wait for your son to grow up, you don't want to miss the moment. You don't want to miss his life now. Now is the time to make those memories which will warm your nights and days when your son has left home and made his way in the world.

Let Advent remind you of that, and may we all prepare our hearts during this Advent season for the coming of Christ at Christmas.

On the Inscrutable Providence of God

Every morning, without fail, I read my two favorite comic strips, "Zits" and "For Better or for Worse." "Zits" is about the trials and tribulations of two devoted parents trying to raise their incredibly typical fifteen-year-old boy, Jeremy. "For Better or for Worse" relates the lives of the Patterson family of Canada. Recently, the cartoonist of "For Better or for Worse" retired, and the papers are now rerunning the twenty-year series. In recent weeks, the mother of the family, Elly, has fought a losing battle with her husband and her five-year-old son over the family's adoption of a puppy. With two children under five, Elly doesn't feel that she needs another "baby" for whom she will be ultimately responsible, knowing that her husband and her son will leave the task of raising the puppy to her. Of course the puppy is so cute that Elly gives in. What Elly doesn't know—and what I'm sure the cartoonist didn't know when she first began the story of Farley, the puppy—is that, in fifteen years, Farley will give his life saving Elly's yet-to-be-born daughter, April, when, as a three-year-old, she falls into the river near their house. April is a late-in-life child. I remember well the strip in which Elly tells her husband she is expecting. With a horrified look on his face, he exclaims, "You're what?" The cartoonist, Lynn Johnson, is certainly no theologian, but as she created the lives of the Patterson family, she unwittingly makes a beautiful case for the providence of God. The puppy, which Elly doesn't want, will become the savior of the beloved daughter, whom Elly does not expect.

The founder of the Xaverian Brothers, Theodore James Ryken, motivated by his profound faith in the providence of God, once said, "The ways of God's providence are often inscrutable but always adorable." On occasion, I have shared with you the words of St. Edith Stein, Sister Teresa Benedicta of the Cross, which I have had on my desk for the last twenty-five years:

> Whatever did not fit in with my plan did lie within the plan of God. I have an ever deeper and firmer belief that nothing is merely accident when seen in the light of God, that my whole life down to the smallest details has been marked out for me in the plan of divine providence and has a coherent meaning in God's all-seeing eyes.

So many things happen to us in our lives which seem not to make sense because we can only see them with the very limited sight of our own experience. How our lives fit into the divine plan is a mystery which will only be revealed to us when we are with God in heaven, but I do think we have glimpses of it occasionally on earth. In 1980, I had the opportunity to teach in England, something I very much desired, but as it turned out, I remained where I was and became the assistant principal. A month later, my mother became very sick, and within a month she died. If I had been in England, I would not have been able to be with my father, my sister and my mother as we went through her sickness and death. Now, I don't think God wills sickness and death. It's simply part of our human condition, but because He is God, He can bring good out of what, to human eyes, seems completely tragic. I've seen this happen so many times.

A boy I had in school years ago wanted nothing more than to attend the Naval Academy. For assorted reasons he didn't make it through his plebe summer. With his dreams seemingly shattered, he went on to obtain his degree in engineering at another school and began working for a company which sent him to Cincinnati. There he met the woman of his dreams, now his wife. Once, when we were talking, he said to me, "If I had gotten my dream of Annapolis, I never would have met my wife. Now I can't imagine life without her. I guess God does know what He's doing."

We are beginning the beautiful season of Advent, my favorite season in the Church's year of grace. The beautiful readings from Isaiah, the longing of the Jewish people for the coming of the Messiah, the willingness of Mary to become involved in a mystery which she could not possibly understand—all of this reminds us that God has a plan which does not unfold in minutes but in centuries. God has more patience than we do! As we wait during Advent with the Church for the coming of Christ at Christmas, let's take the time to remember what the Angel Gabriel said to the Virgin Mary, that nothing is impossible to God.

Farley, the unwanted dog, becomes the savior of the much beloved daughter, and what seems like failure is just God's way of sending a young man to Cincinnati. As Brother Ryken said, "The ways of God's providence are often inscrutable but always adorable."

Happy Advent.

On Advent and Slowing Down

Since I have been a religious for forty-four years, the liturgical seasons of the Church's Year of Grace have very deep significance for me. When I was first diagnosed with cancer in 2006, it was during Lent, and that made a great deal of sense to me. As I was lying in the hospital without two-thirds of my colon, with a colostomy and six months of chemotherapy ahead of me, I realized that the Lord was inviting me to do some "cross time" with him during Lent. At the time, I almost considered it a privilege. If you have had any experience with serious illness and have found yourself in the "medical mill," you realize that waiting is frequently the hardest part of any complicated medical problem. As this school year was beginning, I experienced a second bout of cancer and had three very anxious weeks, waiting for the medical mill to determine exactly what was wrong with me. At first, the doctors thought I might have two different cancers growing simultaneously. After those very long three weeks, I was given the "good news" that it was only one kind of cancer, but that it had spread. During those weeks, I kept thinking, "It should be Advent. I could cope with all of this so much better if only it were only Advent." Waiting is the quintessence of Advent.

One of the contemporary hymns for Advent begins with the words, "Patience, people, for the Lord is coming." To wait patiently galls our American temperament. We are used to instant gratification in so many ways. Instant messaging, text messaging, e-mails, and cell phones which do everything but blow your nose seem to have made waiting a thing of the past, yet, in the major areas of life, there are still things for which we must wait, situations for which there is no instant gratification. Advent is the Church's time—and God's time—to tell us to slow down and to wait patiently for the salvation which God has promised us.

Being an Advent person, I rather resent the anticipation of Christmas which now seems to begin at Halloween. An "Advent person" doesn't want the decorations until the purple of Advent is over.

Advent is an invitation to slow down the pace of your life. Now, I can hear you say, "Really, Brother, how can you slow down the pace of your life when you have to do Christmas shopping, decorate the house and discover the latest electronic toy that your son wants for Christmas?" Nonetheless, I suggest that you find some time during Advent to take time for yourself and to slow the pace. Christmas isn't about the gifts we give to one another. It is about the gift which God has given us in Christ. Take some time to wait for His coming and to remember what a tremendous gift He is.

I'd like to end with my favorite passage in all of scripture, from the Prophet Isaiah:

> But now, thus says the Lord, who created you, O Jacob, and formed you, O Israel: Fear not, for I have redeemed you. I have called you by name: you are mine. When you pass through the water, I will be with you; in the rivers you shall not drown. When you walk through fire, you shall not be burned; the flames shall not consume you. For I am the Lord, your God,

> the Holy One of Israel, your Savior. I give Egypt as your ransom, Ethiopia and Seba in return for you. Because you are precious in my eyes and glorious and because I love you . . . fear not for I am with you.
>
> Isaiah 43: 1–5

Truly, God *is* with us—always. Especially during Advent, He invites us to take time to wait patiently and to remember how very much He loves us. Happy Advent!

Christmas 1995

> For God so loved the world that He gave His only Son, so that everyone who believes in Him might not perish but have eternal life. For God did not send His Son into the world to condemn the world, but that the world might be saved through Him.
>
> John 3: 16–17

A reporter for the *Xavier News* recently asked me about my fondest memory of Christmas. I found it very difficult to choose one memory of Christmas because my mind has been flooded recently with memories. My sister has been cleaning the basement of my father's house and, in late November, she sent me a gigantic box of pictures and mementos of our family. My mother, like most mothers, had saved a record of our family, beginning with my parents' marriage in 1937 and only ending with my mother's death in 1980. There were not only photographs, but report cards and honor certificates which my sister and I had received. Interestingly enough, my mother had saved a certificate which I had received in the fourth grade for proficiency in handwriting. I think she wanted to remind herself that, for one brief moment in my life, I could actually write legibly! As I went through the box, picture by picture and memento by memento, I was overwhelmed by wonderfully warm memories of the love that I experienced from my parents.

My box of memories arrived just as Advent was beginning, and the memories have colored my Advent reflection. In the beginning of his Gospel, St. John tells us that God so loved the world that He sent His only Son to be our savior. Because the Gospel and the Christmas story are so familiar to us, we can so easily fail to grasp the awesome truth they contain. We have all experienced tremendous love within our families, whether that be from our parents, grandparents, siblings, or children. Yet even when we have experienced the most profound of human love, we have not begun to tap the depths of God's love. As beautiful and as wonderful as it is, human love is but a pale reflection of the love God has for each one of us and which He expresses in the tremendous gift of His Son. As we celebrate Christmas this year, wouldn't it be wonderful if we came to realize deeply in our hearts what a tremendous gift of God's love Christ is?

May Christ be born in our hearts at Christmas and may He bless each and every one of us with the tremendous love of His Father and with many warm memories. Merry Christmas!

CHRISTMAS 1998

> They even brought babies to be touched by Him. When the disciples saw this, they scolded them roundly; but Jesus called for the children, saying: "Let the little children come to me. Do not shut them off. The reign of God belongs to such as these. Trust me when I tell you that whoever does not accept the kingdom of God as a child will not enter it."
>
> LUKE 18: 15–18

The Pittsburgh International Airport is a strange setting for a Christmas story. It is one of my least favorite places, and yet I seem to spend an inordinate amount of time there as I fly back and forth to various meetings. In his book *Diary of a Country Priest,* Georges Bernanos writes, "Grace is everywhere." Unfortunately, God's grace is at times so subtle that we don't perceive it. And who would expect God to be alive and at work in the Pittsburgh International Airport?

Serving as it does as the hub of US Airways, the Pittsburgh Airport is incredibly busy. Planes land and take off at an alarming rate, and thousands of people run from gate to gate making connections and meeting friends. In the midst of this confusion sat a disgruntled religious Brother, cursing God and his fate because he had yet again missed his connecting flight. As the Brother watched the passing parade, he noticed a small boy, no more than three years old, standing in a ticket line next to his father. The little boy was obviously fascinated by the airport and the throngs of people all hurrying to and fro, but he wasn't at all frightened because he was right next to his father. When the father and son came out of the ticket line, they seemed to be paying no attention to each other. The father was looking in one direction while the little boy was looking in another. Yet with the trust that perhaps only a child has, the little boy extended his hand up to reach for his father's. At the same time, the father was reaching down for his son. Their hands met and they walked off into the crowd. A simple scene, certainly not extraordinary. It was, nevertheless, a moment of grace for the Brother who witnessed it. Child-like trust is awesome to behold and certainly difficult for us adults and "almost adults" to practice. Such trust is, however, the very essence of Christmas.

On Christmas, we celebrate the great feast of the Incarnation, God becoming man. In the person of Jesus, God has joined hands with us, a loving father extending His hand to His children. What a beautiful lesson we could learn at Christmas if we learned the uncomplicated trust of that little boy in Pittsburgh.

May the good Lord grant us the grace to trust in His unfailing love and may He bless each of us with a happy and peaceful Christmas and a prosperous New Year.

CHRISTMAS 2001

> She had gone one lunchtime into Westminster Cathedral, with its mysterious depths, the bleakness of its unclothed heights, the glimmer of its mosaics, the theatrical yellow arch behind the high altar, the scattered points of glowing gold from the candlestands. She had thought the Cathedral dark, vast, and ugly compared with the patina and beauty of Westminster Abbey; then she had sensed the atmosphere of prayer; there was a coming and going; many people come to pray, not looking for history or beauty but prayer. Suddenly an old man beckoned to her. He was a tramp. She saw him now, dirty, unshaven, unlovely in a drooping old overcoat, his trousers tied with a string. Surely if there is a miracle, that is the miracle? That someone quite ordinary, by some not extraordinary action, can work providence? To find a tramp in the Cathedral was most likely. "One of the good things about a Catholic Church is that it isn't respectable," she had told Richard. "You can find anyone in it from duchesses to whores, from tramps to kings."
>
> FROM *IN THIS HOUSE OF BREDE* BY RUMER GODDEN

Westminster Cathedral, the Catholic Cathedral in the heart of London, is my favorite church. Unlike the Anglican Cathedrals in England, which can seem more like museums than churches, Westminster Cathedral is very much a house of God, a place of prayer. Because it is in the heart of London, visitors to the Cathedral are incredibly diverse. Workers in nearby businesses regularly attend one of the daily Masses while the homeless, so prevalent in London, find a home at the Cathedral as well. I have always been impressed with how reverently the ushers at the Cathedral treat the homeless, some of whom are mentally ill. Even when these people are disturbing the divine services, the ushers treat them respectfully, understanding that they have a perfect right to be there. As Rumer Godden writes, "One of the good things about a Catholic Church is that it isn't respectable. You can find anyone in it, from duchesses to whores, from tramps to kings."

Three years ago, I attended a morning Mass at the Cathedral a few days after Christmas. The Mass was being celebrated in one of the side chapels, and it was very well attended. As I knelt during the canon of the Mass, I became aware of the diversity of the crowd. There were well-dressed professionals, both men and women, and a few women who, if they weren't duchesses, certainly looked as if they could play the part quite well. There were many ordinary men and women, like myself, who were looking for a quiet place to pray, and there were the homeless men and women who appeared to be seeking shelter from the cold December day. I knelt next to one homeless man who appeared to be emotionally disturbed. He was mumbling incoherently but very much aware of the progress of the Mass. He became quiet at the consecration and the elevation of the host and chalice and resumed his mumbling as the priest continued with the Mass. Kneeling there, I recognized that this incredibly diverse assembly of people, gathered to worship at the Cathedral, was a perfect lesson about Christmas. When God became man in the Incarnation, He became part of all of us, the well-dressed and respectable and the less than well-dressed and seemingly less respectable. Everyone in that church on that cold December morning was part of Christ, and Christ was part of us. As Christ became present at that Mass, I'm sure that He rejoiced to see the diversity in His body that morning. Because of the Incarnation, everyone in that Cathedral had a right to be there. While I saw diversity in the crowd, I'm sure Christ saw only the splendor of His Incarnation.

As we celebrate Christmas this year, let's take time to remember the true meaning of the Feast, the true meaning of the Incarnation. There is room in God's heart and in God's holy Church for all of us, saints and sinners, the respectable and the seemingly less than respectable. Let's make sure that there's room in our hearts for all of these as well.

Christmas 2002

> There were shepherds in that region, living in the fields and keeping night watch by turns over their flocks. The angel of the Lord appeared to them as the glory of the Lord shone around them, and they were very much afraid. The angel said to them: "You have nothing to fear! I come to proclaim good news to you—tidings of great joy to be shared by the whole people. This day in David's city a savior has been born to you, the Messiah and Lord."
>
> Luke 2: 8–11

Twenty-seven years ago at Christmas, I visited a former teacher of mine, Sister Anna Catherine, as she lay dying in the infirmary of the Sisters of St. Joseph of Boston. As she came to the end of her life, there was an incredible peace which radiated from this frail, old woman. When I mentioned to her that I was struck by how peacefully she was approaching Christmas and the end of her life, she pointed to a plaque on the wall of her room. It read:

Jesus Christ
Yesterday, Today
The same forever.

As she approached her last Christmas, Sister Anna Catherine knew in Whom she had spent her life believing, and she had learned the truth of the message of the angels on the first Christmas night, "You have nothing to fear."

As we celebrate the great Feast of Christmas, let's remember that Christmas is not about the gifts we give to each other, but about the great gift that God has given to us in His Son. With Christ as our Savior, we, indeed, have nothing to fear. Not weekly terrorist threats nor the ravings of Osama Bin Laden nor the prospect of war can ever triumph over Christ. As Saint Paul reminds us, "In all of this we are more than conquerors because of Him who has loved us." (Romans 8:37)

May the good Lord grant us the grace to trust His unfailing love and may He bless each of us with a happy and peaceful Christmas and a prosperous New Year.

Christmas 2003

> But now, thus says Yahweh, who created you, Jacob, who formed you, Israel: Do not be afraid, for I have redeemed you; I have called you by your name, you are mine. Should you pass through the sea, I will be with you; or through rivers, they will not swallow you up. Should you walk through fire, you will not be scorched and the flames will not burn you. For I am Yahweh, your God, the Holy One of Israel, and your Savior.
>
> Isaiah 43: 1–2

Have you ever noticed that you can determine exactly where a person fits in your life by what that person calls you? To most of the people with whom I interact, I am Brother James or Brother Kelly. To my friends, I'm Jim or Kel, but to my family and to my oldest friends, I'm Jimmy. Last month I was giving a talk to the Parents' Council at Saint John's High School in Shrewsbury, Massachusetts, a school at which I had been stationed in the early 1970s. In the midst of the formality of the talk and reception, the parents, naturally, addressed me as Brother, but my Godson's father is on the faculty at Saint John's and was at the reception. At one point as I was talking with him and with some parents, he called me Jimmy, and I immediately felt the warmth that comes with an old friend calling me by that name. For a moment, all of the parents faded and, by the very mention of my name, I came in contact with a deep friendship of thirty-two years standing. In the Isaiah passage which forms the epigraph of this letter, when God tells us that he calls us by name, I think he calls us by that name which most resonates in our heart, the name that the people who love us the most call us. I hope that, when I finally meet God in heaven, he is going to call me Jimmy.

As we celebrate Christ's birth, we celebrate the fact that, through Christ, God has become intimately involved with our lives, that, through Christ, God has adopted us as his sons and daughters and calls us by name. Saint Paul tells us that Christ's Incarnation gives us the right to call God Abba, which literally means Daddy. Since we can speak to God so affectionately, we can be sure that he does the same for us.

As we rejoice at Christmas and at the great gift whom God has given us in his Son, let us also rejoice that we have a God who calls us not just by name, but by that name which speaks lovingly to the deepest recesses of our heart.

May you and your family have a very happy Christmas and a blessed New Year.

Christmas 2004

> "Joseph, son of David, do not be afraid to take Mary home as your wife, because she has conceived what is in her by the Holy Spirit. She will give birth to a son and you must name him Jesus, because he is the one who is to save his people from their sins." Now all this took place to fulfill the words spoken by the Lord through the prophet: "The virgin will conceive and give birth to a son and they will call him Emmanuel," a name which means God is with us.
>
> Matthew 1: 21–24

When a young colleague of mine was appointed the first lay headmaster of a Xaverian Brothers' school, I gave him the advice that I think every new headmaster of a Catholic school needs to hear. I told this novice headmaster that he always needed to remember that the school is not his. It is God's, and the success of the school is far more dependent on the grace of God than it is on any action or omission of the headmaster. Now, I am not always good at heeding my own advice, but I have discovered over my years as a school head that, when I remember Mount Saint Joseph is God's school and not mine, things go along much more smoothly and with much less anxiety. In Rumer Godden's novel *In This House of Brede,* a relatively young nun is elected Abbess of a large Benedictine monastery. Overwhelmed by the responsibility of her election, she flees to the Abbey Church, kneels and prays, "Dear God, I can't, so You must." I have always thought that those seven words constitute the perfect prayer.

How modern our Christmas story is: an unwed teenage mother and a young man who is told not to be afraid to marry a woman who is carrying a child which isn't his. The angel tells Saint Joseph that Mary will give birth to a child who will be "God with us." Through the mystery of the Incarnation, God entered our history in a definitive way, and, in Christ, God is with us at every moment of our lives. If we can only remember that, how easy life would be, even in its most difficult moments! I know that, on days when Mount Saint Joseph seems overwhelming to me, if I remember that the school is God's and not mine, I am consoled and find the strength to continue. The prayer of the Abbess becomes my prayer on those days. No doubt you have days like that as well. At the most difficult times of life, God can seem distant, but what we celebrate at Christmas reminds us that God is never distant, that he is "God with us" every moment of our lives. If we can only remember that, we can celebrate Christmas every day of the year.

Mr. Fitzpatrick and I wish you and your family a very Happy Christmas and a Blessed New Year. May God, born for us at Christmas, be with you now and always.

Christmas 2005

> For God so loved the world that, in the fullness of time, He sent His only begotten Son, so that everyone who believes in Him may not be lost but may have eternal life.
>
> John 3: 15–16

As I write this letter, it is the first week of Advent, and I have just begun the retreat which will end my Sabbatical. I grew up in the pre-Vatican II Church where we were taught that we had to earn God's love by our good behavior. As I have grown older and, hopefully, wiser, I have come to realize that God's overwhelming love is an unconditional gift which He gives us, not because we have earned it, but because He is our Father who loves us beyond words. Nothing that you or I do, good or bad, can add or subtract from God's love for us. It is a pure gift.

During the course of my Sabbatical, I have been listening to a song called *Come As You Are,* by the Australian singer Paul Gurr, in which there is a line where God speaks to the soul, saying, "Each time you fail to live by my promise, why would you think I'd love you the less?" It makes sense. You are well aware of your son's faults and failings, but his faults and failings and his insensitivity at times, to you and to others, do not change one iota the love you have for him. In fact, your awareness of his faults and failings can deepen your love for him. So it is, with God and with us. Sin is real, both in the world and in us, but our sinfulness does not change God's love for us, just as a child's sinfulness does not change a mother's love for the child.

Of course, there are tremendous implications of God's love. He loves each one of us without exception. That means that he loves people like Osama bin Laden and the terrorists who have harmed so many innocent people. Perhaps that is what Jesus meant when he said that we have to love our enemies and pray for those who persecute us. We have to love our enemies as God loves them. Certainly that's no easy task.

In San Antonio, I have met a very wise and holy priest who gave me this definition of purgatory: He said, "I think that when I get to heaven, I am going to be so overwhelmed by God's tremendous love for me and so ashamed of how little I have loved Him in return. That shame will be my purgatory." If that is not theologically correct, it ought to be!

At Christmas, we celebrate the great sign of God's love for us, the Incarnation. God gives us his only Son to share our humanity and to teach us how great is the Father's love for us: "God so loved the world that, in the fullness of time, He sent His only begotten Son." As we celebrate this Christmas, let's not forget that the greatest gift that is given to anyone at Christmas is the overwhelming gift of God's love. May each one of us and our families receive that gift with grateful hearts as we celebrate the birth of God's Son.

May you all have a very Happy Christmas and a Blessed New Year.

CHRISTMAS 2006

Every other Saturday, my good friend, Brother Giles, calls me from Kentucky. We were stationed together at St. X and lived together during my years in Kentucky. He called me occasionally, but not frequently, before I became sick last March, but since then he has been a very faithful telephone correspondent. He always ends our conversations by saying, "I love you, buddy." To that I respond in kind. One of the things that has most struck me since I became sick last March is how often now people tell me that they love me. These are people whom I've always known loved me, but they never expressed it very often. Friends and family are now far more expressive in their affection than they were before I got sick. I wonder what it is about cancer, or any serious sickness, which compels us to realize that we need to tell people that we love them. Whatever the cause, I am most grateful.

While we might, at times, hesitate to tell people that we love them, our God never hesitates. That's what Christmas is all about. The birth of Christ is one big "I love you" from God and, more often than not, we let this "I love you" pass, not really believing what a wonderful gift it is.

During my illness, the image of the Good Shepherd has become very precious to me. In the early months, my daily prayer was simply to remind Christ that He is the Good Shepherd and I am the very sick lamb whom He has in His arms. That image comforted me, and as I began to grow healthier, I became more and more convinced of how very much God loves me. We believe in a loving and forgiving God who loves the world so much that He gave His only begotten son for our salvation.

Christmas is God's great love-feast for His creation. Let us rejoice in His love and remember that He asks us to share that love with all whom we meet in our life's journey. May the Good Shepherd, born for us at Christmas, bless the Mount and all Mount families with health, happiness and peace. Merry Christmas!

Christmas 2007

This past summer, it was my privilege to attend the 26th General Chapter of the Xaverian Brothers which was held in Bruges, Belgium, the city in which we were founded by Theodore Ryken in 1839. The Chapter began with a retreat at the Carmelite Church on Ezelstraat in Bruges, the church where our Founder and the earliest Brothers prayed. The retreat was a very moving experience for me and for all the Brothers assembled at Chapter. We were able to pray in the same church where our Founder and his first companions must have spent so many hours praying and hoping for the success of the foundation. The first house of the Congregation, only a short walk from the church, is now an abandoned ruin, but even in its youth, the house was in one of the poorer sections of Bruges. The fact that the house is now a ruin also moved me because I think it speaks so eloquently to the poverty which our Founder and the Brothers endured. In December of 1839, with his Congregation only six months old and struggling for existence, our Founder spent his first Christmas as a Brother in a poverty which was very much reflective of Bethlehem. Ryken had nothing but his faith as he began our Congregation. Cold and hunger were his lot. Of the earliest Brothers, only Ryken persevered. The destitution of the Congregation at its beginnings was too much for the others to bear. During his first Christmas he had nothing but his faith in the Providence of God to sustain him, but sustain him it did.

As we prepare for Christmas, we so often lose ourselves in the hustle and bustle of buying gifts, decorating, and planning for Christmas dinner. How easy it is to forget the meaning of the feast as we experience the materialism of our culture. As we celebrate this Christmas, let us remember that it is about God's greatest gift to us, the gift of his Son, a sign of a love for us that is so great that it almost goes beyond our human capacity to understand. Ryken understood, and it was this understanding of God's love for him and God's Providence which sustained him through the poverty of our foundation.

My prayer this Christmas is that we will all, in some small way, come to understand the tremendous love of God made manifest in this feast. May Christ, born for us in Bethlehem, bless and keep close to Him all members of the Mount Community.

Merry Christmas!

Christmas 2008

> In the tender compassion of our God the Dawn from on high shall break upon us to shine on those who dwell in darkness and in the shadow of death and to guide our feet into the way of peace.
>
> Luke 1:78–79

When Zechariah, the father of John the Baptist, finally recognizes the miracle which God has worked in his wife Elizabeth, conceiving as she does when an old woman, he bursts into the joyful canticle which the Church calls *The Benedictus* and which religious recite every day as part of morning prayer. Zechariah realizes that his son will be the precursor of the Dawn breaking upon us to shine on those who dwell in darkness and the shadow of death.

We think of miracles in terms of the spectacular and the extraordinary, such as an old woman like Elizabeth conceiving a child, but when you think about it, we are surrounded every day by ordinary miracles where God speaks to us very clearly of His love and grace. One of the happier memories of my career is of a teacher coming into my office with an incredible smile on his face to tell me that his wife was pregnant after years of not being able to conceive. Their son, and then his brother who came along eighteen months later, were certainly unexpected miracles for their parents. After a recent junior retreat, Miss Coyne, the retreat director, told me that the transformation which she saw in one boy over the course of the retreat had to be as close to miraculous as anything she had ever seen. Recently Mrs. Van Bavel, who is on maternity leave, came in with her month-old son, Andrew, and as I looked at this tiny baby asleep in his mother's arms, I was struck by what a miracle life is. Every day, miracles surround us if only we will pay attention!

In the hustle and bustle of our world, we can lose sight of the incredible miracle that Christmas is. The almighty and all-powerful God has become a baby, asleep in his mother's arms, vulnerable and fragile. How often we stand on our dignity and don't want anyone to take advantage of us. In the Incarnation, God certainly did not stand on His dignity, so great was His love for us.

As we celebrate Christmas this year, let's look for the ordinary miracles in our lives even as we contemplate the extraordinary miracle of God becoming man. May the good Lord, born for us at Christmas, bless all of us with health, happiness and peace.

Christmas 2009

On Christmas, in the dark and very cold days of December 1940, as the British awaited the full brunt of Nazi fury, King George VI broadcast to England and to the British Empire one of the more memorable speeches of his sixteen-year reign:

> A new year is at hand. We cannot tell what it will bring. If it brings peace, how thankful we shall all be. If it brings us continued struggle, we shall remain undaunted. In the meantime I feel that we may all find a message of encouragement in the lines, which in my closing words I would like to say to you: "I said to the man who stood at the Gate of the Year, 'Give me a light that I may tread safely into the unknown.' And he replied, 'Go out into the darkness, and put your hand into the Hand of God. That shall be to you better than any light, and safer than a known way.'" May the Hand of God guide us always.

The Incarnation and birth of Christ which we celebrate at Christmas is not mere metaphor. In its most profound reality, in Christ, God is putting His hand into ours to hold us firmly and to guide us rightly. Wars, terrorist attacks, and the effects of the terrible economy can never triumph over God's tremendous gift to us in Christ. Years ago, my spiritual director, knowing how difficult my restless nature found it to sit quietly in prayer, suggested that when I go for walks, I hold my right arm as if it were grasping the hand of Christ and that my prayer consist of a conversation with this very dear friend who loves me more than I can imagine. At first I thought it seemed rather silly, but as I practiced this form of prayer, I realized that Christ was, in fact, holding my hand. I wasn't imagining His presence. His presence was very real.

As we celebrate this Christmas, let's try to realize more deeply that God has, in Christ, put His hand in ours as a guardian and a guide and that He will never let go. Good tidings of great joy indeed!

Epilogue

If you have found anything helpful in this book, I would ask that you pray for the author. As you have probably deduced from some of the letters, I have been on a four-year journey with cancer. That journey has entered a rather serious stage. I am, however, a very lucky man. For the past four years, I have been enveloped in the prayer of those who love and care for me. I can't tell you how consoling I have found that. God makes his love known to us in the people who love us, and God has been very present to me through these people.

I have been a very fortunate man in my vocation. I have taught boys who, in many ways, taught me more than I taught them. I've had the good fortune to love every school at which I have been missioned, including the faculty and staff at each school with whom I have been privileged to serve. Most importantly, I love all of the boys whom I've met and taught over the last forty years. The late Brother Lambert always said that he hoped the one thing his "old boys" would remember about him is how very much he loved them. I can honestly say that I have that same hope for my "old boys." Whether I actually taught them in class or they were simply boys in the three schools over which I have presided as headmaster, I hope that they know how very much I love them. Whether I've known every boy whose hand I've shaken as I've presented him with his diploma doesn't matter. I've loved them all. At the

Mount, I know most of the students in the graduating class because Mount boys are so friendly and they make sure you know who they are. Still, at graduation, Mr. Fitz whispers in my ear the names of those boys who go by a name other than the name on their diploma. Regardless, I love them all simply because they are Mount boys. We call them "Mount Men," but, in this Xaverian Brother's mind, they are all boys, boys on a journey to manhood, but boys nonetheless. It has been my great spiritual privilege to walk with them and with their parents on that journey.